HEARTS AFLAME WITH HOPE

Volume Two

Peter-Julian Eymard & John Henry Newman

Hearts Aflame with Hope

VOLUME TWO

Peter-Julian Eymard & John Henry Newman

MICHAEL GAUDOIN-PARKER

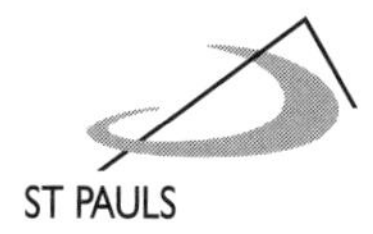

ST PAULS

Library of Congress Cataloging-in-Publication Data

Gaudoin-Parker, Michael L.
   Eymard & Newman / Michael Gaudoin-Parker.
      p. cm. — (Hearts aflame with hope ; v. 2)
   "ISBN 10: 0-8189-1343-6"
   Includes bibliographical references and index.
   ISBN-13: 978-0-8189-1343-3
   ISBN-10: 0-8189-1343-6
   1. Peter-Julian Eymard, Saint. 2. John Henry Newman, Blessed. 3. Christian saints—
Biography. 4. Hope—Religious aspects—Christianity. 5. Lord's Supper—Catholic
Church. 6. Lord's Supper. 7. Christian life—Catholic authors. 8. Christian life. I. Title.
II. Title: Eymard and Newman.
   BR1720.A9G38 2012
   270.2092—dc23
                                    2011040737

Produced and designed in the United States of America by the
Fathers and Brothers of the Society of St. Paul,
2187 Victory Boulevard, Staten Island, New York 10314-6603
as part of their communications apostolate.

ISBN 10: 0-8189-1343-6
ISBN 13: 978-0-8189-1343-3

Printing Information:

Current Printing - first digit	1	2	3	4	5	6	7	8	9	1 0

Year of Current Printing - first year shown

2012	2013	2014	2015	2016	2017	2018	2019	2020	2021

For Miguel

"May the God of hope fill you
with all joy and peace in believing,
so that by the power of the Holy Spirit
you may abound in hope" (Rm 15:13).

[A]ll mankind is of one Author, and is one volume; when one man dies, one chapter is not torn out of the book, but translated into a better language; and every chapter must be so translated; God employs several translators; some pieces are translated by age, some by sickness, some by war, some by justice; but God's hand is in every translation, and his hand shall bind up all our scattered leaves again for that library where every book shall lie open to one another.

John Donne[i]

You read, my brethren, in the lives of Saints, the wonderful account of their conflicts, and their triumphs over the enemy. They are… like heroes of romance, so gracefully, so nobly, so royally do they bear themselves. Their actions are as beautiful as fiction, yet as real as fact. *John Henry Cardinal Newman*[ii]

Be content that you are not a saint, even though you realize that the only thing worth living for is sanctity. Then you will be satisfied to let God lead you to sanctity by paths that you cannot understand. You will travel in darkness in which you will no longer be concerned with yourself and no longer compare yourself with other men. Those who have gone by that way have finally found out that sanctity is in everything and that God is all around them. *Thomas Merton*[iii]

Table of Contents

Foreword

When I received the invitation of Father Michael Gaudoin-Parker to write the foreword to his new work presented in a four-part series, my initial reaction was that I was too busy to undertake this task. But once I realized that he was writing about hope and the Eucharist I quickly changed my mind. What caught my interest immediately was the way he was connecting hope and the Eucharist; specifically in the lives of men and women we have come to admire and to love.

In our life journey we all need help to illumine the way forward, and as Christians that Light which is Jesus Christ reaches us in many different ways. One way is through the lives of our ancestors in the faith. These are the women and men who have journeyed with hope in their hearts and who have centered their faith in the Person of Jesus Christ – a hope that is nourished in the celebration of the Paschal Mystery. In a world that is often desperately and hopelessly in search of the transcendent in all the wrong places, come along those giants in the faith who live their lives by hope and whose example we all need in order to remind us of our rootedness in a community of faith at the Lord's Table.

Here is another rich spiritual contribution by Father Michael Gaudoin-Parker to his already numerous writings, such as *Heart in Pilgrimage, A Window on the Mystery of Faith, The Real Presence through the Ages,* and *Hymn of Freedom.* In his latest work the reader will discover, in addition to inspirational descriptions of how real people have lived in hope through the Eucharist, abundant food for meditation on hope and the Eucharist which the author examines in his Prelude. As in his other books the author provides the reader with a wealth of resources by way of quotations from a wide range of ancient and recent writings from theologians and poets to Church documents.

I was struck by the apt choice of the persons for the volumes in this presentation. It draws our attention to the fact of how their Christian experience was essentially the same, despite the diversity of their historical situations, temperaments, and manner of responding to the challenges presented by the Gospel. This choice likewise calls us to reflect on a key notion in the Eucharistic teaching at the dawn of Christianity, that which the Apostle Paul expressed at different times: "Because there is one bread, we who are many are one body, for we all partake of the one bread" (1 Cor 10:17); or again, "There is one body and one Spirit, just as you were called to one hope that belongs to your call, one Lord, one faith, one baptism, one God and Father of us all, who is above all and through all and in all" (Eph 4:4-6). This truth about seeking relationship in diversity, implied in the lives of the persons the author considers here as protagonists of hope, provides a powerful incentive for building community that is not polarized by political allegiances or divided over sectarian causes and elements of prejudice and discrimination. Rather, it impels us in the ongoing endeavor and indispensable task of working towards Christian unity, communion with Christ and with one another.

There are times when it is good to change one's mind. This time I was pleased that I had. Change, after all, is involved in the process of conversion, a theme to which the author refers in his treatment of the spiritual journey towards hope illustrated by people whose lives were inspired and nourished by the Eucharist, that reality at the center of the Christian community causing the amazement of adoration, renewal of outlook and transformation in orientation. In this sacramental encounter, we too, like them, find our hearts set aflame to face and venture into the future with confidence, as the two disciples discovered along the road to Emmaus at their meeting with that Stranger, who turned out to be none other than the Risen Lord

Jesus. I discovered in Father Michael Gaudoin-Parker's four volumes material for many a meditation on a subject, hope and Eucharist, which will not only inform my mind but also help to conform my prayer as well as my lifestyle with its decisions and expectations to "the riches of the glory of this mystery, which is Christ in you, the hope of glory" (Col 1:27).

V. Rev. Fr. NORMAN PELLETIER, S.S.S.
Provincial Superior of the Blessed Sacrament Congregation,
St. Ann's Province, U.S.A.

Preface

"The Eucharist is at the root of every form of holiness, and each of us is called to the fullness of life in the Holy Spirit. How many saints have advanced along the way of perfection thanks to their Eucharistic devotion!... Holiness has always found its center in the sacrament of the Eucharist " (Benedict XVI, Apostolic Exhortation *Sacramentum Caritatis* [Feb. 22, 2007], n. 94). Based on this conviction, Father Gaudoin-Parker presents in this four-part series eight persons who not only have lived the Eucharist in their daily lives, but also have seen the extensive implications of this mystery in terms of hope and communion. These were eight pilgrims, who along their journey encountered the mysterious fellow-traveler of Emmaus (cf. Lk 24:13-35), to whom they opened both their life and the significance of their search: "*We had hoped* that he was the one to redeem Israel..." (Lk 24:21). In this phrase "*we had hoped...*" there is encompassed the image of our lives in which hope has become difficult, if not impossible. Myths, in fact, have vanished; ideologies have been shattered; the future is fearful; depression has become a social concern and all the heart-warming expectations for springtime have been frozen by unforeseeable frosts.

"*We had hoped...*" Yet, never entirely extinguished, that desire to "hope beyond hope" (Rm 4:18) bursting out of humankind's heart has no other basis than that pertaining to Christians: faith. Only by clinging to the Lord "who is faithful" (cf. Dt 7:9) does hope become possible. Because of this the Apostle Paul proclaims many times to the Christians of his time: "Christ Jesus [is] our hope" (1 Tm 1:1);

or, even more clearly: *Christ is our hope because he is the Crucified and Risen One who lives forever*. The specific feature of our faith is indeed hope in the resurrection, in that love stronger than death, in eternal life. But, where is the "pledge of future glory" (*pignus futurae gloriae*), the source of this hope?

The answer to this question is found in the liturgical experience of the Eucharist, because in it human hope has its foundation, is renewed and grows from the presence of the Lord who comes! It is in the liturgy that there takes place an encounter between the Lord who comes and his people who seek and await him: here is that face to face encounter between God and his community, the Church; the embrace of the Lord and each believer.

Right from its origins, the Eucharist was celebrated in an *eschatological perspective*: in this, in fact, not only is there the memorial of Jesus' Pasch, but also there is prefigured the Banquet of the Kingdom of God, where communion between Christ and the redeemed will be fully realized. This eschatological character of the Eucharist is well brought out in the Eastern and Western Christian liturgies, which after the Institution Narrative in different ways proclaim both the memorial of the death and resurrection of Jesus, and also of his coming at the end of time, that is, the *Parousia*. It is sufficient to recall the acclamation that we usually proclaim in the Latin liturgy: "We proclaim your death, O Lord, and profess your Resurrection until you come again." The Eucharist is the source of hope because in it the crucified and risen Lord is "he who comes": there he explains the scriptures, as for the disciples of Emmaus, and he reveals himself under the signs of bread and wine. For this reason we can proclaim: "Blessed is he who comes in the name of the Lord" while we anticipate the memorial of the banquet of the Kingdom when we will sit at table with Jesus and he, according to his promise, will come and serve us (cf. Lk 12:37).

To draw hope from the celebration, however, it is necessary to pay attention to some important underlying principles.

Above all, the Eucharist requires the gathering together of the "scattered children of God" (Jn 11:52) in the same place around the Lord who has been lifted up from the earth and glorified. The very fact of being gathered together every Sunday for the Eucharist points towards the hour of the glorious coming of Jesus Christ, it manifests prophetically that eschatological encounter, which in a fragmented and divided world as ours ought to imbue hope and joy in us. Despite the apparent simplicity of our celebrations, every Sunday we carry out a prophetic gesture that offers hope to us and to all people, since we become united in communion in the hope of welcoming the Lord who comes. We cannot lose a sense of this awareness of communion that was so well expressed in the primitive Church: "As this broken bread, once dispersed over the hills, was brought together and became one loaf, so may your Church be brought together from the ends of the earth into your Kingdom." (*Didaché* 9,4.) The only way that the assembly can spread such a hope is by being oriented towards Christ who comes.

In the second place, we are gathered on a very particular day: Sunday, "the day of the Risen Lord" and "a day of the Lord's coming," a promise of the Kingdom that is coming about. The 20th canon of the Council of Nicea (325) directs Christians who are gathered for the Sunday Eucharistic celebration not to kneel down, but to remain standing: they, in fact, are journeying towards the Kingdom, as men and women "risen" with Christ, freed from every kind of servitude, in expectation of entering into God's "rest."

Finally, even the way in which we celebrate should make visible and audible the fact that the Eucharist is the source of hope. Even when the Eucharist is celebrated in communities often comprising elderly and fragile persons, it is a font of hope because this shows the Church in the sanctifying reality of little ones and the poor, the suffering who long to meet the Lord: they pray and celebrate the liturgy to hasten the coming of him who "will bring about justice" for all those in the world who have endured affliction and injustice.

In a word, Father Gaudoin-Parker's approach in bringing together the witness of eight pilgrims of hope points to the truth that

Blessed John Paul II stated, namely, that the celebration of the Eucharist always "spurs us on our journey through history and plants a seed of living hope in our daily commitment to the work before us" (Encyclical Letter *Ecclesia de Eucharistia* [Apr. 17, 2003], n. 20).

ARCHBISHOP PIERO MARINI
President of the Pontifical Committee
for International Eucharistic Congresses

Acknowledgments

I take this opportunity to express my gratitude especially to Father Norman Pelletier, S.S.S., for generously agreeing to write the foreword of this present four-part work. I am also deeply indebted to Archbishop Piero Marini, the President of the Pontifical Committee for International Eucharistic Congresses, for writing the preface, in which his theological, liturgical, pastoral and spiritual insights contextualize the rich teaching of the pilgrims of hope considered here.

My gratitude would be incomplete without recognizing other persons as well for their advice and constant encouragement: Professor Justin Taylor, S.M. of the École Biblique in Jerusalem, Dr. Stratford Caldecott of Oxford, Louis Volpe and Miguel Andrade.

Abbreviations

AA   Various authors

AAS   *Acta Apostolicae Sedis*

AV/KJV Authorized version/King James Version

B & O   Burns & Oates

CCC   *Catechism of the Catholic Church* [ET] London: Geoffrey Chapman, 1994

CL   *Christifidelis laici* (December 30, 1988) Pope John Paul II, Post-synodal Apostolic Exhortation

CT   *Catechesi tradendae* (October 16, 1979) Pope John Paul II, Post-synodal Apostolic Exhortation

CUA   The Catholic University of America

CUP   Cambridge University Press

CV   *Caritas in Veritate* (June 29, 2009) Pope Benedict XVI, Encyclical Letter

CWS   The Classics of Western Spirituality

DCD   *De Civitate Dei*

DCE   *Deus caritas est* (December 25, 2005) Pope Benedict XVI, Encyclical Letter

DM   *Dives in misericordia* (November 30, 1980) Pope John Paul II, Encyclical Letter

DLT   Darton, Longman & Todd

DO   *The Divine Office. The Liturgy of the Hours According to the Roman Rite*, London/Sydney/Dublin: Collins/E.J. Dwyer/Talbot, 1974

DS   Denzinger-Schönmetzer, *Enchiridion Symbolorum*, Herder, 1967

DV   *Dei Verbum* (November 18, 1965) Second Vatican Council, Dogmatic Constitution on Divine Revelation

DViv   *Dominum et Vivificantem* (May 18, 1986) Pope John Paul II, Encyclical Letter

EE   *Ecclesia de Eucharistia* (April 17, 2003) Pope John Paul II, Encyclical Letter

ET   English Translation

EV   *Evangelium vitae* (March 25, 1995) Pope John Paul II, Encyclical Letter

FC   *Familiaris Consortio* (November 22, 1981) Pope John Paul II, Post-synodal Apostolic Exhortation

FR   *Fides et ratio* (September 14, 1998) Pope John Paul II, Encyclical Letter

GS   *Gaudium et spes* (December 7, 1965) Second Vatican Council, Pastoral Constitution on the Church in the Modern World

ICS   Institute of Carmelite Studies

LG   *Lumen gentium* (November 21, 1964) Second Vatican Council, Dogmatic Constitution on the Mystery of the Church
NEB   New English Bible
OUP   Oxford University Press
Pb   Paperback
PO   *Presbyterorum ordinis* (December 7, 1965) Second Vatican Council, Decree on the Ministry and Life of Priests
PPS   *Parochial and Plain Sermons*
PUG   Pontificia Universitas Gregoriana
RH   *Redemptor hominis* (March 4, 1979) Pope John Paul II, Encyclical Letter
RM   *Redemptoris Mater* (March 25, 1987) Pope John Paul II, Encyclical Letter
RSV   Revised Standard Version
SC   *Sacrosanctum concilium* (December 4, 1963) Second Vatican Council, Constitution on the Sacred Liturgy
S.C.   Sources Chrétiennes
SCar   *Sacramentum Caritatis* (February 22, 2007) Pope Benedict XVI, Post-synodal Apostolic Exhortation
SCM   Student Christian Movement
SD   *Salvific doloris* (February 11, 1984) Pope John Paul II, Apostolic Letter
SPCK   Society for Promoting Christian Knowledge
SpS   *Spe salvi* (November 30, 2007) Pope Benedict XVI, Encyclical Letter
S & W   Sheed and Ward
ST   *Summa Theologia*
VD   *Verbum Domini* (September 30, 2010) Pope Benedict XVI, Post-synodal Apostolic Exhortation
VS   *Veritatis splendor* (August 6, 1993) Pope John Paul II, Encyclical Letter

PRELUDE

Raising of Hope Beyond Hope

Human life is a journey. Towards what destination? How do we find the way? Life is like a voyage on the sea of history, often dark and stormy, a voyage in which we watch for the stars that indicate the route. The true stars of our life are the people who have lived good lives. They are lights of hope. Certainly, Jesus Christ is the true light, the sun that has risen above all the shadows of history. But to reach him we also need lights close by – people who shine with his light and so guide us along our way.

Pope Benedict XVI[1]

The faith that I love the best, says God, is hope.

Charles Péguy[2]

The supernatural vitality of hope overflows, moreover, and sheds its light also upon the rejuvenated powers of natural hope. The lives of countless saints attest to this truly astonishing fact. It seems surprising, however, how seldom the enchanting youthfulness of our great saints is noticed; especially of those saints who were active in the world as builders and founders. *Josef Pieper*[3]

At a time when loss of the past has cost so many their sense of the future and the destruction of continuity has deprived them of hope, we may, in all due reverence, restate the words of the apostle in 1 Cor 13:13: "So faith, hope, love abide, these three; but the greatest of these is hope." For where there is no hope, love is a thing of the moment and faith is an idle fancy. But with hope, faith may dare to love, even amid the changes and chances of this present life, and to look forward to the fulfillment of perfect love in the presence of God. *Jaroslav Pelikan*[4]

I

Was it a call to revive hope that rang out on May 16, 2009, when the largest and heaviest bells in the world, those of Liverpool's Anglican Cathedral, pealed out the music of John Lennon's song "Imagine there's no heaven"? What message of hope was announced in this song? But, in a sense the lyrics didn't matter; it was just the sound of music that drew hundreds of people together in a nostalgic moment recalling a folk hero who has become for many a legendary prophet of world harmony and peace. Words have oftentimes only divided people, made them bitter, caused wars. Even the words of religion that are meant to offer "good news" have played a part in distracting people from the task of "Living for today... Living in peace... Sharing all the world" – the hopeful ideals expressed in the last line of each stanza of Lennon's song. Whatever was his intention or message in writing this song, however its words are interpreted, it is legitimate to raise the question: What is the *basis* of the hope expressed? Apart from this question, there is another: What *kind* or *image* of concord and sharing of universal brotherhood is envisaged?

When John Lennon's song made its debut in 1971, it certainly caused a stir: it made people think; it provoked controversy about whether this was another example of the subversive "flower-power" Hippie subculture sweeping through the world; it upset a complacent attitude about reward in the hereafter as offering a flight from focusing on "today" as the day of salvation; it was also heard as fostering a "live just for today" attitude – that is, the kind of pleasure-seeking materialism and hedonism sometimes associated with the Latin poet Horace's phrase *carpe diem* ("seize the day"). The context of Horace's phrase, however, is not primarily about promoting a desire for delighting in the luster of the present moment, but about the issue of time and the uncertainty of knowing the deep significance and outcome of life's ephemeral, scintillating moments: "Seize the day, trusting as little as possible in the future."

In a post-modern culture many people have grown weary and disheartened by complicated, abstract philosophical arguments about the meaning of being and nothingness, or indeed, about the impossibility of saying anything significant regarding human existence. George Steiner took up the challenge thrown out by those who ask: "Is there anything in what we say?"[5] In a stimulating essay he argued that implicitly in every work of art, especially music, the human imagination dreams of making "an absolute leap out of nothingness."[6] Imbued with a conviction steeped in the religious tradition of Judaism, Steiner goes further in claiming that, in fact, no statement or question or human endeavor to communicate is ultimately meaningless, but grounded in the revelation of God's presence. This signifies that all attempts on the part of human beings to say or do anything reach out to touch the mystery of the Other; they act as a hospitable host to the primordial Source of being; they as it were translate and show, albeit imperfectly, the elusive "Face" of the divine.

The scope of Steiner's conjecture is vast insofar as it is not restricted merely to the possible truth-bearing function of art, such works as Mozart's *Don Giovanni*, Shakespeare's *Hamlet*, or Picasso's *First Steps*. If the term "art" is understood in a global sense as encompassing every work carried out by human beings, then recognition is made possible about their capacity to pierce through a cloud of unknowing so as to participate in the realm of creativity that pertains, strictly speaking, to God. If this daring claim of Steiner is right about God not being ultimately absent, albeit implicitly underwriting the order of creation and the logic and language-events of human history, then nothing is lost, every endeavor contributing to the betterment of the world and to the construction of culture is never in vain, the yearning in the human heart for regaining paradise is validated, heaven is not a figment of mere imagination, a distraction that deserves to be discarded. Every human experience is indeed shot through with the provocation to abide in the hope to seek God's presence.

It has been remarked, however, that today in the Western world many people have lost not only a sense of God, but also interest in seeking a sense of future through recourse to the biblical roots of their rich religious tradition.[7] The historian Jaroslav Pelikan observed that the Christian message has not changed, but rather the mood of modern times, in which there is "a loss of appetite for the future, a failure of the capacity to hope, a paralysis of expectation." He attributes the fact of the fundamentals of the Christian teaching on hope being under attack to credence being easily given to the notion of progress, the "secular counterpart" to "the Christian expectation of the life of the age to come." "The secular doctrine of progress," he adds, "may be seen as the attempt to affirm the Christian hope of the future without the Christian faith in the past."[8] Because of this the processes of history are regarded thus as self-redeeming and as moving inevitably toward the achievement of their inherent goal without need for any belief in the redemptive incarnation or hope of sharing in the resurrection of Jesus Christ.

This outlook on history can be traced back at least to the Age of the Enlightenment, the catch-cry of which was the optimistic, but cold challenge "Dare to know!"[9] Long before Nietzsche or Marx, religion was debunked by thinkers such as Montesquieu, Voltaire, and Diderot, who regarded it as the root cause of social divisions, obscurantism and bigotry. A thoroughgoing this-worldly attitude, that came to be called "secularism," "secularist" and "secularization," spread like wildfire in recent centuries regarding the introduction of new approaches to education, morality and freedom that threatened to replace the beliefs and value system inherited from Christian tradition.[10] The nineteenth century was marked by a growth of individualism, agnosticism, skepticism and doubt. As a direct consequence, there came about a general cooling off in the attitude of many people to the traditional practices of religion and a growing indifference to matters of faith. A striking example of a reaction to this is seen in the writing of Dostoevsky, the great Russian representative of the Orthodox Church's spirituality in the religious drama of the nineteenth century. While describing himself as "a child of unbelief and doubt," a state in which he expected to remain until his death, he spoke of the cost to persevere in a certain "burning *desire* to believe" in Christ.[11]

Dostoevsky's most distinguished English contemporary, Newman sought to dispel the skepticism that under various guises had been darkening faith in Victorian England, a period that has been called an "Age of Doubt." He clearly perceived as he stated near the beginning of his work on the development of Christian doctrine: "to be just able to doubt is no warrant for disbelieving."[12] The phenomenon of doubt can be regarded, thus, in another light as masking a deeply religious spirit of searching for what Christian hope signifies. Tennyson's "honest doubt"[13] is an instance of there being more faith abounding than some books about the nineteenth century acknowledge. Rather, such honesty about the mystery of God indicates faithfully and humbly clinging more to God than a self-assured arrogance does in holding onto one's own point of view. As Pascal had earlier pointed out, the existence of doubt needn't mean either an absence of faith or an abandoning of searching for God, for, despite all perplexity and darkness, comfort can be taken in the very fact that searching for God implies somehow having found him.[14] Furthermore, having faith doesn't – and mustn't – dispense one from searching deeper into the mystery of God revealing his desire to unite human beings in his life of Communion. The tension between doubt (whether experienced by unbelievers or the faithful) about the ultimate sense of life and an insatiably ongoing questing "soul-desire" constitutes and, indeed, highlights the religious vocation, the eschatological God-orientation of humankind. Rather than in any way quashing this tension, the place of hope is valuable and indispensable insofar as it realistically acknowledges the need to transcend merely time-bound humanistic perspectives and preoccupations. These latter only lead to a "dead-end" state of anxiety of not knowing, which is endemic to agnosticism, practical atheism, or escapist indifference that paradoxically takes up a "positionless position" or irresponsible attitude of carelessness regarding the past, present or future, typical of what pertains to the nonchalant relativism prevalent today. Faith on the other hand always entails a seeking to understand, a deepening of the basis to live in hope.

Conversion-curve towards being in communion

Individualism and subjectivism which were promoted by some nineteenth century philosophical theorists became characteristic features of the last century. In various writings, notably his essay "The Poison of Subjectivism," C.S. Lewis brilliantly unmasked the fallacies of selfishly pursuing individual goals as destructive of the very communal nature of being human.[15] Christian hope on the other hand maintains and intensifies that passionate thrust and concern for sharing life in a community of meaning. It awakens, prophetically interprets, creatively stimulates and raises the common experience of confronting the significance of life and death to an entirely new level by challenging human beings to be turned around to look to Christ, who came to reveal an abundance of life through his Paschal Mystery. This turning around or conversion to him, while certainly implying a radical change of conduct or way of living, is based on something far deeper than that of adopting a system of ethics or morality. It involves taking on his way of looking at and loving life, and even more profoundly, that of being conformed to him. This is the radical orientation of the newness presented in the New Testament, particularly as expressed by the Apostle Paul's teaching on being renewed in the image and likeness of Christ, whose "form" of holiness, that is, relatedness and participation in God's glorious design, enables all persons to realize their true worth by responding to God calling them to living worship in faith, hope and charity.[16] St. Paul's doctrine about this is magnificently illustrated in his rich imagery of all things being recapitulated in Christ (cf. Eph 1:10).

The Eucharistic Mystery brings out an experiential integration and transformation of every aspect of human experience. In celebrating this mystery the community of faith is impelled to pass beyond all that divides individuals and dichotomizes their understanding and appreciation of God's call to share hope in the fulfillment of his design and purpose for the unity or communion of people and all creation through Christ in the joy of the Spirit. In a word, the Church's celebration of the Lord's Paschal Mystery sacramentally holds together memory and hope, actualizing, setting in motion and giving an ever new impetus to the dynamic of human life together in community. This celebration of the Risen Lord's presence and action in mystery was succinctly described by the Second Vatican Council as

> a memorial of his death and resurrection: a sacrament of love, a sign of unity, a bond of charity, a paschal banquet in which Christ is consumed, the mind is filled with grace, and a pledge of future glory is given to us.[17]

The relatedness of all human experiences to their eternal significance as fulfilling the design of God is the perspective proclaimed and celebrated by the Christian community at every Eucharist, which, to repeat the cardinal phrase of the Second Vatican Council, is "the source and summit of the Church's life and mission." Being gathered by the Holy Spirit in this central event of their lives, the Christian people are led out of the narrow confines of their immediate time-bound constricted circumstances and freed from the thickets of their individual preoccupations and concerns, which they are enabled to perceive in a new light so as to appreciate them as being part of a broader horizon. In no way does this imply that the experiences of the present temporal condition are without value or that there is a loss of their importance through an otherworldly attitude being assumed by Christian believers. Rather, through encountering the action of the Risen Savior-Lord in Eucharistic worship, all things become recognized as pregnant, so to speak, with their true potential. This is the truth-bearing quality revealed by the Eucharistic Celebration. The ordinary of daily experience – signified by the bread and wine, transformed by the action of the Father's gift of the Spirit of his Word and the Christian community's prayer (cf. 1 Tm 4:4f.) – becomes recognized for what it truly is: the foretaste of what hitherto "eye has not seen, nor ear heard, nor what can be imagined" (1 Cor 2:9). By growing in this hopeful awareness, the Christian community is brought to its senses and becomes impelled to the worship of God in thankful praise so as to recognize that, to quote the poet Hopkins' words, "the world is charged with the grandeur of God." This recognition entails a true conversion of heart, a transformation that, dare one say, is no less wonderful than the conversion of the elements of bread and wine into Christ's Body and Blood, the entire significance of which exists for no other purpose than to enable people through the renewal of their minds to offer themselves, all that they have and are as a living sacrifice of spiritual worship (cf. Rm 12:1-2).[18] The renewed perception of all things through sharing the sacramental sacrifice of the new and eternal covenant in Christ's Pasch makes the Christian community truly Eucharist-hearted – that is, converging in a dynamic conversion-movement of thanksgiving and praise for Christ "in you the hope of glory" (Col 1:27).

This expression of St. Paul must be understood in relation to his intense and profound awareness of the newness of Christian existence, for which he coined a new phrase "in Christ" to designate it. This "you" in Col 1:27, while certainly involving a personal sense of relationship to Christ, is given by the Apostle's Greek as a plural, personal pronoun (‘υμιν), not singular. The significance of Paul's emphasis on the communal corporate relatedness of Christians with Christ would be lost if his expression were interpreted only in a psychological, individual and subjective sense. Moreover, the Pauline teaching about the existential communal dimension of the worship offered throughout Christian living (cf. Rm 12:1-2) has an eschatological openness, which, nevertheless, is realized in a concrete way because grounded in the Eucharistic "sacrifice of praise" that consolidates the faithful in the conversion-curve towards being in communion.

The spirituality of being in the communion of hope

In experiencing the Eucharistic covenant of God's loving kindness Christ's faithful become impelled by hope. For through sharing

Christ's Paschal Mystery they become contemporaries with all those who have gone before them "marked with the sign of faith." This contemporaneity sacramentally entails an openness to the mystery of being hope-filled in its widest and deepest dimensions, which participate in comprehending with all the saints the height and depth, the breadth and width of God's outreach to humankind in Christ (cf. Eph 3:18f.). In the words of a former great Anglican Archbishop of Canterbury, Michael Ramsey:

> The deepest significance of the past is that it contains reflections of what is eternal. Saintly men and women of any age belong to more than their own era: they transcend it. Therefore openness to heaven is necessary for a Christian… Openness to heaven is realized in the communion of saints in deliberate acts of prayer and worship. But it is realized no less in every act of selflessness, humility or compassion: for such acts are already anticipations of heaven in the here and now.[19]

Despite the tendency towards a linking together of people in a classless society promoted by the doctrines of Marx and Engels; despite the last century's awareness of the importance of communitarian ideals and endeavors to realize dialogue and democracy through modern educational methods; despite the rapidly growing technological means of communication; a sense of isolation is the common experience of many people, who at a deep personal level feel unconnected and unable to relate, and therefore frustrated in not understanding or in being misunderstood. This experience results from being at cross-purposes with one another – whether at their work with colleagues or in relations with friends, or at home between parents and their children (especially as the latter begin to desire to express their independence and identity), or between spouses themselves.

The hope for building community thus endangered by a widespread breakdown in communication is further jeopardized in the modern world of "virtual" possibilities presented by technological expertise, possibilities that seduce the imagination into believing that one creates a space of escape from the sense of impotence experienced in ordinary existence. This flight into the "virtual" surrenders a sense of responsibility to shape one's being with others. Moreover, it evades the deeper responsibility to God, who calls and offers the possibility through grace to live in relational communion with him and with others. By fleeing into an artificial environment and "virtual" space, for example, provided by computer games such as "Second Life," the genuinely creative energies of many youth – and not only of them! – become dissipated in an indulgence of the desire for diversion in a pseudo-relational miasma of cyber "a-temporality," so that commitment to the tasks of the present moment is ignored. W.B. Yeats' poignant lines would seem to have a chilling ring of prophecy regarding the scenario of this situation, although to call it "situation" seems inappropriate and contradictory:

> Things fall apart; the center cannot hold…
> The ceremony of innocence is drowned;
> The best lack all conviction, while the worst
> Are full of passionate intensity.[20]

Nevertheless, despite the disappointments resulting from relational dysfunctional and unrealized aspirations and ideals, despite various escape routes from responsibility to be committed, the thrust to go on seeking a deeper genuine sense of hoping cannot be stifled.

The theme of the 50th International Eucharistic Congress in Dublin, "Communion with Christ and with one another," has, thus, a poignant relevance, since

> it speaks to the heart of our identity and mission particularly at a time when there are fundamental shifts in patterns of communication and human relationships. The more traditional interpersonal networks and social ties

diminish, the more there is need to find new models of relating at regional, national and global levels.... In God's plan, the Church is to be a sign and instrument of uniting people with God and with one another. As Tertullian, one of the early Church writers put it, "One Christian alone is no Christian." In the Eucharist we discover the genetic code of communion that is at the heart of the Church's identity. It is in meditating what Eucharistic communion means that we realize how the brokenness in communion of the body of Christ strikes at the heart of the Church's evangelizing mission.[21]

This theme of communion has been the focus of the Church's understanding of its ecclesiology highlighted by and since the Second Vatican Council, since its significance, as fostered, celebrated and lived in an ecclesial environment, is essentially oriented towards realizing the ultimate scope and purpose (*telos*) of human existence: sharing the faith-based hope of being at-one, attuned in God's love disclosed through the Paschal Mystery of the Risen Lord Jesus Christ. Recognition of this purpose is a presupposition, a prelude to engaging in the theme-song of existence, hope, through which humankind is in concert with God's design in the universe. As the Catholic poet laureate, John Dryden, put it:

> From harmony, from heavenly harmony,
> > This universal frame began:
> > From harmony to harmony
> Through all the compass of the notes it ran,
> The diapason closing full in Man.[22]

In a post-modern culture, in which attention is paid to narratives and meta-narratives, it is conceivable that the lives – the "stories" – of the saints would hold an appeal. But, these are not merely accounts. They present real lives that are harmoniously related to and relate the wonderful works of God:

> Their music goes out through all the earth,
> their words reach to the end of the world.
> (Ps 19[18]:4 - NEB)

Insofar as God's Word is proclaimed, listened to and obeyed, our words and ritual actions and, indeed, the whole of our lives reveal and radiate and echo Christ, the Word of Life. The Word itself is the Christian community's only fitting, explicit and prayerful response to God's loving gift communicated in the redemptive Incarnation. The whole of the Christian community's life is thanksgiving or *eucharist* in response to the Word of God.[23] Christians, as St. Athanasius put it, are appropriately said to be *wordified*, that is, become the Word in virtue of participating in the divinized newness of communion through being in Christ by the working of God's Holy Spirit.[24] Because of being in communion with Christ, Christians bear witness to the Word's Spirit of holiness resonating in them.[25] This witness is in deed, in living charity, not in "wordiness" or, as St. Ignatius of Antioch put it: "It is better to keep quiet and be, than to make fluent professions and not be."[26]

The witness and teaching of the persons presented in this four-part series illustrate much more than the optimism entertained by the Age of Enlightenment. They celebrate what the poet Alexander Pope realized, namely, that hope is a blessing from God enabling humankind to aspire to what is eternal:

> Hope springs eternal in the human breast;
> Man never is, but always to be blest.[27]

Sharing in the communion of saints

Holiness, one of the marks characterizing the identity of the Christian Church as the Second Vatican Council emphasized, is possible and realizable particularly in a communal or ecclesial context of the entire people of God.[28] The joy pertaining to this holiness is constituted and deepened by working together in hope to realize the transcendent, eschatological dimension of human existence – that dimension which even here on earth opens humankind to welcome the coming of God's kingdom, the "new creation."[29] This new creation is already within reach, as Pascal stated confidently:

> The Christian's hope of possessing an infinite good is mingled with actual enjoyment as well as with fear, for, unlike people hoping for a kingdom of which they will have no part because they are subjects, Christians hope for holiness, and to be free from unrighteousness, and some part of this is already theirs.[30]

The truth of these words is reflected in the lives of the persons considered here as signs of encouragement to humankind to hope. The pages of this series focus on their journey of conversion towards greater union with Christ through his gift and mystery of the Eucharist, of which they offer an extended catechesis and celebration. Through being nourished and strengthened by Christ's Paschal spirituality, these persons – some of whom are canonized saints – are outstanding models of holiness. They responded to and were thoroughly imbued by the transformative transcendent perspective coming from God's gift of the theological virtue of hope. In considering their lives it is well, however, to heed Newman's sound words about avoiding to "chop up a Saint into chapters of faith, hope, charity and the cardinal virtues," for books of this kind "do not manifest a Saint, they mince him up into spiritual lessons."[31]

The cluster of essays in this series begins with Augustine of Hippo, whose story of conversion and teaching offer a paradigm of the theme of Christian hope. The rigorous and unremitting search of this great African Father of the Church for truth led him to delve profoundly into the revealed Word of God. Although some of his writings have been criticized for containing elements of pessimism, nevertheless, it would be churlish to deny that his overall influence on Christian theology and spirituality remarkably shaped Western society into a culture of hope, for his fundamental teaching can be summed up as emphasizing the primacy of God's loving outreach to humankind in grace. The chapter on Francis of Assisi presents that much loved saint, whose perspective about living became entirely changed through his encounter with the Crucified Savior: in this memorable meeting he learned to deepen his practical commitment to serving the poor in this world and thus to build up the Church as a community of hope oriented towards looking forward confidently to the Lord, who will ask every person to give an account of fidelity to his real presence in the needy.

The nineteenth century French priest Peter-Julian Eymard in this volume is an example of a person, who, captivated by contemplating God's love for the world manifested in Christ's gift of self in the Eucharistic mystery, unstintingly dedicated himself to what he perceived was the crucial problem of humankind, namely, the need to discover how communion with Christ as worshippers of God in spirit and truth empowers people to become united in the hope of realizing a genuine renewal of society.[32] The chapter on John Henry Newman, whose holiness has recently been officially recognized in his beatification, has its place next insofar as this illustrious convert's journey clearly shows the vital importance of fidelity to conscience as being essential to discovering the meaning of hope.

In the third volume of the series, the chapters on two discalced Carmelites, Thérèse of Lisieux and Teresa Benedicta of the Cross (Edith Stein, the convert Jewish martyr of Auschwitz), attempt to bring out the value of contemplative life, as the great reformer of the Carmelite order Teresa of Avila emphasized, in sustaining and deepening a genuine Christian understanding of hope.

Like the martyr of the Nazi persecution, the piece on Archbishop Oscar Romero of El Salvador in the fourth volume deals with his heroic witness for bringing about a better world against the inhuman situation of social injustice and violence menacing his people. In the following chapter, the stand of Dorothy Day through her undaunted inspiring struggle for peace and her endeavors in setting up the Catholic Worker movement is instanced as a sign of human transformation encompassed in the perspective of the Gospel of hope, proclaimed and celebrated in the Eucharist, the Sacrament of the Paschal Mystery par excellence.

The "Postlude" is an attempt to gather some of the threads that made the hearts of those persons considered in this four-part series aflame with hope; it offers no more than a glance at the powerful message spread abroad by those two great witnesses of hope, Pope John Paul II and Mother Teresa of Calcutta, whose entire lives pointed to Christ, calling people to do whatever he asks: like the Blessed Virgin Mary – the Mother of the Church and "Woman of the Eucharist" – they perceived that in the new wine shared in the Lord's Paschal gift of his Eucharistic cup is contained a foretaste of the joy of the nuptial banquet of God's kingdom of the eternal life of communion (cf. Jn 2:1-11; 17:3).

Inspired and sustained in following the pathway traced out by the Risen Lord's mystery of life through dying to self, the lives of the persons referred to here illustrate how they became transformed into transparent and coherent signs of hope for their contemporaries as well as for us today. Others may well have been included: Jean-Marie Vianney, the humble parish priest of Ars, whose dedicated ministry as a confessor brought countless persons back to Christ; Mary MacKillop, Australia's first saint, who, even though suffering misunderstanding on the part of ecclesiastical authority, remained loyal to her calling to serve the poor; or the Irish laywoman Edel Quinn, whose cause of canonization is still being examined, who showed an intrepid missionary spirit as an envoy of the Legion of Mary to East Africa; or James Alberione, a saintly Italian priest whose zeal for spreading the Gospel led him to found the Society of St. Paul, the Daughters of St. Paul, three other religious congregations and secular institutes, which proclaim hope to the masses in a vitalizing apostolate through employing the most advanced technological possibilities of the media.

Much earlier there were countless others: Patrick, who evangelized the peoples of Ireland; Benedict of Nursia, who launched the great monastic movement that educated Europe in a civilization of love; Catherine of Siena, whose important role in bringing the papacy back to Rome turned the course of events in history; Francis Xavier, who after joining Ignatius of Loyola, founder of the Jesuits, became an ardent apostle of the Far East; the two Spanish Carmelite reformers, Teresa of Avila and John of the Cross. All such persons, like those represented through this four-part series, form a vast cloud of witnesses of hope stretching, indeed, even beyond Christianity (cf. Heb 12:1). They penetrated the heart of God's Word articulated fully in Christ, a message which is

> not only "informative" but "performative." That means: the Gospel is not merely a communication of things that can be known – it is one that makes things happen and is life-changing. The dark door of time, of the future, has been thrown open. The one who has hope lives differently; the one who hopes has been granted the gift of a new life.[33]

The Spirit-filled Word in the transforming sacramental sacrifice of Christ has nourished and impelled people from different cultural backgrounds down the ages to lay claim to the God-given yearning to seek what every human being has the right to realize: the truth of holiness that made them genuinely human as members of the fellowship or communion of divine love. They were set free from fear or disheartenment through believing and trusting in the Risen Lord Jesus (cf. Jn 8:32) and thus surrendered themselves to follow him, the Lamb, wherever he goes (cf. Rv 14:4). They allowed themselves to be transformed by the grace of God, freely cooperating with him who, as C.S. Lewis put it, "made it a rule for Himself that He won't alter people's character by force."[34] Their hearts aflame with hope for communion with Christ and all people redeemed through his Paschal Mystery joyously manifest to us today "the riches of the glory of this mystery, which is Christ… the hope of glory" (Col 3:27).

Imagining the steps towards heaven on earth

An image may perhaps better depict all that is attempted here in words. Words, after all, do little better service than those that describe the poet John Keats' experience as "straining at particles of light in the midst of a great darkness."[35] Pablo Picasso's painting *First Steps* illustrates an observation made by St. Peter-Julian Eymard:

> When a mother wishes to teach her child to walk, she goes before him/her, holds out her arms and as the child approaches the mother goes back a step and so on until the child has become confident to walk without being held. Jesus likewise treats a soul he loves.[36]

Although these words don't exactly express the same scene depicted by the Spanish artist, the images communicated have identical points of reference: the intimacy of family relations, the delicate process of learning and experiencing reciprocal trust, the parental excitement tinged with a sense of risk, but also delight in witnessing their child's development in which they play a crucial part. Moreover, the imagery is imbued with implicit hope about a child's faltering and vulnerable "First Steps" onto the world's stage. (The darkness from which a child is guided by a mother symbolized for Picasso the situation under the Nazi occupation of Paris in 1943, when the painting was produced.) The hope to emerge from darkness to light can be recognized in the parenting desire of God, who in launching each person into existence hopes that he/she will take surer, confident strides toward finding and freely following that calling in life leading to the experience and expression of proper qualitative worth. Picasso's startling image may be interpreted as God tenderly guiding each person forward through the Church just as in Eymard's description he waits eagerly like a mother with outstretched arms to welcome and embrace each human being. This hope-filled waiting on the part of God is the predominant theme of Charles Péguy's great poem, *The Portal of the Mystery of Hope*:

God put his hope in us. He took the initiative.
He hoped that the least of the sinners,
That the tiniest of the sinners would at least
    work a little for his own salvation…
He hoped in us, will it be said that
    we didn't hope in him…[37]

Another image of hope may be that of a delicate thread woven by God together with his other gifts of faith and love throughout the whole fabric of human life. This thread can be seen as holding together the lives of the persons looked at here. It passes through and unites their multiple human experiences, as it does through ours: desire, dynamism of motives, searching for truth, questioning, reflection and decision-making, hesitations and fears in facing suffering, even torture and eventually death – that climactic challenge to abandon one's self confidently into the hands of God, as Jesus did on the Cross.

Without the mystery of the Cross, no hope is ultimately possible. This is why the Church's liturgy salutes it as "unica salus" and we reverence it, saying: "We adore you, Christ, and praise you, because by your holy Cross you have redeemed the world." Through it Christ united himself with humankind in love, embracing all phases of suffering that are traceable ultimately to the loveless condition of sin, which results from the pride of disobedience to God. Through it he was raised up by God's Spirit (cf. Rm 8:11; Ph 2:5ff.) and thus became the world's Savior who draws all to himself (cf. Jn 3:14f.; 8:28; 12:32). Through nothing other than the light of this same mystery of the Cross we are interiorly purified of selfishness and our perspective becomes clarified. Through the Cross, that powerful symbol which like a compass radically orients the course of our existential journey, we become aware that solidarity with the world is integral to being called and sustained by God's grace to holiness. In the hope of realizing this we become more deeply responsible for living with hearts aflame with hope moving towards that great communion of relatedness in God's eternal life of love.

When interacting with the circumstances constituting the flow of history in which we can't but be involved, we would be neither daunted or overwhelmed by the task at hand, nor dismayed by our weakness, weariness or even failures, if we read everything, as many other men and women did before us, in the light of the hope-giving trust engendered by the Paschal Mystery of Christ's life, death and Resurrection. Through this hope we are saved.

That this salvific goal is realizable and no mere daydream about heaven on earth is the aim of presenting the persons remembered in this four-part series titled *Hearts Aflame with Hope*. Their lives, their struggles, their teaching offer us encouragement in reaching this goal, towards which we are enabled through participating in the sacrifice of the Risen Savior-Lord's Paschal gift and mystery of love in the Eucharist. His loving sacrifice of the Cross, like all Christian imagery for that matter,[38] is the key to answering the questions raised above at the beginning. It is very *basis* of the reality of all hope; it shows clearly the *kind* of hope that ultimately matters. It is, as it were, the prelude of the Church's great hymn of thanksgiving and praise to God for hope beyond hope, the *Te Deum*, which concludes with the words:

> May your mercy always be with us, Lord,
>   for we have hoped in you.
> In you, Lord we put our trust: we shall not be put to shame.

In the Post-communion prayer of the Eucharistic Celebration for the solemnity of All Saints, the Christian community expresses gratitude and praise to God for his wonderful deeds of grace manifest in the lives of those who have been drawn in hope towards him, the acknowledged "fountain of holiness." The prayer continues:

> Fill us with your love as we set forth from this table on our
> earthly pilgrimage, and bring us at the last to your heav-
> enly banquet. Through Jesus Christ our Lord. Amen.

In drawing to a close this introduction about the persons featured in the pages that follow, it seems appropriate to recall the words of Pope Benedict XVI who points to the Virgin Mary as the "star of hope" for all humankind:

> With her "yes" she opened the door of our world to God himself; she became the living Ark of the Covenant, in whom God took flesh, became one of us, and pitched his tent among us (cf. Jn 1:14).[39]

Michael L. Gaudoin-Parker
Assisi, February 4, 2011[40]

3

"With the Eucharist… I understand heaven, its glory and its bliss."[41]

Peter-Julian Eymard

(1811-1868)

Disciple and Apostle of the Eucharist

Holiness is nothing other than the gift of one's personality.
Antoine Blanc de Saint-Bonnet[42]

Everyone paints himself with his word, especially with his inner word, and it has been well said that the whole of man is but the expression of his inner word. Now, Reverend Father Eymard wrote down this interior conversation he had with God, with himself and with his friends, in those hours of solitude and peace that the saints keep for themselves amid the tumult in which their lives inevitably take place, and we have to hand some of these precious pages.
Abbé Alexandre Seymat[43]

It is when I turn to Christ, when I give myself up to His Personality, that I first begin to have a real personality of my own.... There are no real personalities anywhere else.... How monotonously alike all the great tyrants and conquerors have been: how gloriously different are the saints.
C.S. Lewis[44]

Christ came to gather together the scattered People of God (cf. Jn 11:52) and clearly manifested his intention to gather together the community of the covenant, in order to bring to fulfillment the promises made by God to the fathers of old (cf. Jr 23:3; Lk 1:55, 70)... every Eucharistic celebration sacramentally accomplishes the eschatological gathering of the People of God. For us, the Eucharistic banquet is a real foretaste of the final banquet foretold by the prophets (cf. Is 25:6-9) and described in the New Testament as

> "the marriage-feast of the Lamb" (Rv 19:7-9), to be celebrated in the joy of the communion of saints.   *Pope Benedict XVI*[45]

The significance of the fact cannot be missed that at the end of the first session of the Second Vatican Council Pope John XXIII took great delight in adding the name of Peter-Julian Eymard to the Church's official list of canonized saints, that "phalanx of those resplendent stars," particularly because "the Eucharist was the characteristic feature and dominant idea of his entire priestly activities that were centered on Eucharistic worship and apostolate."[46] This recognition on the part of the Church points him out as an outstanding witness and sign of hope for our times. More recently Pope Benedict XVI mentioned this founder of the two religious congregations (for men and women) among those saints who from the beginning of the Christian Church to our own day have drawn their fullness of life in the Spirit from the Eucharist.[47] The Visitors' Book at the house in La Mure where Eymard was born and died contains an entry written by the famous organist composer of Notre Dame in Paris, Olivier Messiaen, who expressed his delight that this saint gave pride of place to devotion to the Blessed Sacrament. Peter-Julian Eymard was one of the many persons who were inspired and raised up by God in the nineteenth century to dedicate themselves to movements for the renewal of society through a radical rekindling of Eucharistic fervor.[48]

From sermons, conferences and the personal notes that Eymard made during his retreats throughout his life, as well as from his voluminous correspondence, much insight can be gained not only about the path of his spiritual growth, but also about the spirituality current in his time.[49] Not all the texts are of equal value, some being not more than jottings, others more complete, while others again having been somewhat touched up by some of Eymard's devoted, rather over-enthusiastic followers.[50]

In order to situate and assess properly St. Peter-Julian Eymard's revitalizing mission in the Church, however, it is important to recall something of the historical and social context of the age in which he lived – that which was in the immediate aftermath of the Enlighten-ment and the French Revolution, which had failed to deliver a sense of genuine hope for humankind under the promise of progress. As a consequence of these events, rationalist tendencies, political unrest and instability, social upheaval, as well as anti-ecclesiastical feelings were rife. The nineteenth century saw a general cooling off of the traditional practices of religion and indifferentism to faith. Father Eymard noted that this was particularly the case among men of the "irreligious bourgeoisie."[51]

The climate of faith at Lyons

The city of Lyons bore scars of the above-mentioned two events. It was here that Father Peter-Julian Eymard met various dedicated persons during his ministry as a member of a newly founded religious congregation, the Society of Mary. Attracted by the simplicity of this congregation's Marian spirituality Eymard joined its ranks after a few years pastoral work as a diocesan priest in the country parishes of Chatte and Monteynard in the diocese of Grenoble, for which he was ordained a priest on the ninth Sunday after Pentecost, July 20, 1834. The Venerable Jean-Claude Colin, the Founder of the Marist congregation,[52] welcomed the new recruit on August 20, 1839, the Feast of St. Bernard of Clairvaux, that great devotee of the Blessed Virgin Mary.

At Lyons the zealous young Marist's spiritual and social aware-ness was formed through association with the parish of Saint-Nizier, where he was brought into direct contact with the dual character of Lyons' Catholicism, summed up well as follows:

> Saint-Nizier looked across the Saône River up to the heights above the cliffs where the chapel of Fourvière, Lyon's sanctuary dedicated to the Virgin Mary, watched over the city below. Action and reflection seemed to be facing each other across the river.[53]

This complementary interaction of action and contemplation that Eymard found there in a balanced, practically minded atmosphere played a part in preparing him towards fulfilling his own mission of attending to people's deepest spiritual needs in the light of Christ's revelation of hope for humankind. The apostolic thrust of Christian charity at Lyons was nourished by a deep vein of faith and mysticism, the spiritual roots of which are traceable to its Johannine heritage passed on through the teaching of its martyr bishop St. Irenaeus. This second century Church Father's often-cited sentence may be taken as offering a magnificent résumé of the ultimate scope of human hope for that fullness of eternal life revealed by Christ (cf. Jn 10:10; 17:3): "God's glory is in humankind fully alive; but this life consists in the vision of God."[54] Eymard was imbued with Irenaeus' teaching about the purpose of human existence being to reign with Christ through faithfully serving him: *cui servire regnare est.*[55]

Eymard found a kinship of ideas and sentiment with the philosopher Adolphe Blanc de Saint-Bonnet after receiving a copy of the latter's book on the problem of suffering, *De la douleur.*[56] Blanc de Saint-Bonnet challenged the prevailing tendency of hard-headed rationalism and positivism in France. He was one of those great spirits of the nineteenth century, around whom was formed the so-called 'mystical School of Lyons,' a spiritual hearth from which a not-insignificant contribution shaped by a Christian perspective radiated to literature and political theory.[57] A deep and lasting friendship sprang up between the two men and Blanc de Saint-Bonnet had an important influence on Eymard's own later spiritual development.[58]

Frédéric Ozanam (1813-1853) must have also been known to Father Eymard and the work of this great apostle of charity must have deeply impacted his sympathy for the plight of the socially deprived, for whom he sought a spiritual answer to their problems. Ozanam is most remembered for founding in 1833 the charitable lay association, the St. Vincent de Paul Society, when only twenty years old as a student of Law and Literature. He was beatified by Pope John Paul II in Paris in August 1997. Eymard would certainly have heard about him through his brother, Charles-Alphonse Ozanam, who was for some time a Marist confrere, and through Father Le Prevost.[59] A little-known fact about this zealous apostle is that in 1839 he published a brilliant thesis on the Italian poet Dante.[60] His academic career took him to the heights at the prestigious Sorbonne University in Paris, where he obtained the chair of foreign literature. Because of the sharp criticism of his political liberal views, he was forced to withdraw from public life in his last couple of years to devote his energies more completely to promote the Society of St. Vincent de Paul. Ozanam was a prophet of his times. His qualities of an intellectual honesty, idealism and deep Christian sense of values were no doubt stimulated and brought to practical maturity through contact with some of the foremost thinkers of the day, Chateaubriand and Montalembert, with whom he was associated in the Catholic revival movement in France.[61] During the days of the 1848 riots, which swept through most European countries,[62] he joined forces with Henri Lacordaire, the famous Dominican preacher of Notre Dame, Paris, in starting the publication *Ère nouvelle* that proclaimed a new epoch in Catholic social teaching.

The revolutions that occurred in 1830 and 1848 didn't leave Lyons unaffected, this city being especially a center of growing industrialization that brought to the surface deep rifts in society due to a diffusion of working-class radicalism. The charitable workhouses (called *providences*) in the parish of Saint-Nizier, such as that of the silk workers, were among the targets of attack. These institutions were a hub of sundry benevolent works – soup kitchens for the down-and-outs, hospices for the sick and dying, homes for the handicapped, orphans, elderly and girls "at risk." These places were considered as fostering an unjust and repressive situation that exploited the employees from the lower classes – mainly women and orphaned children. A revolt of the silk workers in Lyons touched the life of Father Eymard, who dared to venture out while the mobs were being incited to rampage and pillage especially religious houses and churches. When seeing the clerical figure they rushed to throw him into the river Rhône. But, he was saved from this by a workman who stopped his colleagues on recognizing this exceptional helper and friend of the workers. Instead, Father Eymard was escorted back triumphantly to the Marist residence.[63]

The parish of Saint-Nizier was a nucleus of intense zeal in support particularly regarding the missionary endeavors of the Society of Mary in Oceania in the South Pacific. New Zealand benefited from this missionary thrust and became one of the principal fields of the Marist Fathers' activity.[64] The flame of this missionary concern was no doubt fanned by the letters and reports from many heroic missionaries in these far-flung lands, to which they had set out as faithful witnesses to Christ's Gospel to the poor, not like some who earlier had supported Spanish colonial exploits in the Americas. Accounts of these apostolic persons' 'adventures' in Oceania were published in a slim blue magazine that appeared regularly every two months by the society of the Propagation of the Faith.[65] This association had been set up in 1820 through the zeal of a woman of extraordinary faith, Pauline Jaricot, whom Father Eymard had met and often visited to encourage the prayer group gathered by her at "Loretto", her home near the great basilica of the Blessed Virgin Mary rising above Lyons at Fourvière.

Among those missionaries to Oceania was a Marist martyred on the island of Futuna, St. Peter Chanel, whom Father Eymard mentioned with pride in two of his letters.[66] He adds a post-scriptum to another letter about news received of the martyrdom of another Marist in New Caledonia, Brother Blaise Marmoiton, whose words he cites: "Why be afflicted? We are only exchanging this life for a better one."[67] On his entry into the Society of Mary, where he encountered an intense spiritual climate favoring missionary zeal, the enthusiastic young Eymard's prayer was focused on two themes: Jesus in the Blessed Sacrament and the desire to fulfill life's greatest hope – for heaven, where the vision of God will be realized. Already during his first retreat as a Marist novice he prayed fervently to be "the first Marist *Martyr*."[68]

In the course of his ministry, in which he was called upon to fulfill responsible positions such as direction of the Third Order of Mary, he felt drawn to follow his calling to found the Congregation of the Blessed Sacrament. This eventually entailed taking a most difficult decision to leave the Society of Mary.[69] He, nevertheless, would insist that he remained a Marist at heart,[70] and near the end of his life he gratefully acknowledged that it was to the Virgin Mary that he owed his vocation as a priest and his mission to be an apostle of the Eucharist.[71] While the Eucharist was the dominant passion of his whole life, it is noteworthy that this was closely linked to and marked by an intense Marian devotion.[72] He called the Blessed Virgin "Queen of the Cenacle" and at the end of his life his final tribute was to give her the title "Our Lady of the Blessed Sacrament."[73] His appreciation of Mary's role within an ecclesiological and Eucharistic perspective can be compared to the Church's teaching today.[74]

Compassion for the deepest hungers of people

Becoming aware of the deepest need of people, namely, that hunger for God, Father Eymard realized that a faith-inspired hope could only be rediscovered through a return to the Eucharist. An example of his sensitivity to the spiritual crisis of the day is seen in a letter he wrote to one of the members of the lay association of the Third Order of Mary, which he was closely involved in setting up. The following words outline his diagnosis of the dire situation and its solution:

> I have often reflected upon remedies for this universal indifferentism that seizes in a frightening way so many Catholics, and I find only one: the Eucharist, the love of Jesus Eucharistic. The loss of faith comes from the loss of love; darkness, from the loss of light; the glacial coldness of death, from the absence of fire. Oh, Jesus did not say: "I came to bring the revelation of the most sublime mysteries", but rather, "I came to cast fire upon the earth;

and my whole desire is to see it enkindle the universe"
(Lk 12:49). Light this divine fire all around you, Madame,
and you will rejoice the heart of our Lord.[75]

A few months later Eymard reiterated to the same person his conviction about the Eucharistic love of Emmanuel (God-with-us) being the
unique and sure means to reverse the growing loss of faith in France
and Europe, adding that when a Eucharistic spark is in a person's
heart no more is needed, since this is the seed of divine life that will
grow and blossom into all the virtues. [76] Convinced of this he was
eventually moved to avail himself of the kindness of his friend Father
Touche[77] to take to Pope Pius IX a letter in which he expressed his
insight about the need for a religious congregation that would have "a
perpetual mission of praying at the feet of Jesus Christ in his divine
Sacrament... the greatest of mysteries."[78] Pius IX greatly favored
this, as Touche assured Eymard, who was much anguished by the
reluctance of Father Favre, Colin's successor as Superior General, to
sacrifice so valued a priest even temporarily to launch this proposed
work. Father Eymard was thus faced with the dilemma of either re-
nouncing his part in it or leaving his beloved Marist family.

Prior to laying his project before the pope, however, his conviction about the Eucharist being the remedy for the irreligious spirit
mushrooming in France had been growing through his association
with persons promoting the movement of Eucharistic piety, such as
the nocturnal adoration society in the South of France or the extension of the Society of Reparatory Adoration to Lyons. His conviction
became particularly confirmed and intensified by personal spiritual
experiences on three crucial and most significant occasions: while
carrying the Blessed Sacrament in the Corpus Christi procession in
the parish of St. Paul in Lyons on May 25, 1845;[79] while praying at
the Blessed Virgin Mary's shrine at Fourvière on January 21, 1851;[80]
and, while offering his thanksgiving after Mass at the college of La
Seyne-sur-Mer on April 18, 1853. The last two events especially
reassured him more deeply about the need for a religious congre-

gation devoted specifically to adoration of the Eucharist. After his experience at Fourvière, in a long letter to Father Colin he set down his thoughts about the need to care for people's spiritual needs by forming a group "for men the same as what is being established for women, a body of men for reparatory adoration"; this group would have lay associates in cities to share in perpetual adoration.[81] After much soul-searching about his motives and his role in founding the work, his perseverance obtained permission from his Marist superiors to go to Paris to make a retreat of discernment and to seek ecclesiastical authorization for his project.

From his arrival in Paris on the eve of the Ascension until just after Pentecost his sojourn was not without trials and anguish. Then, on May 13, 1856, the Tuesday after Pentecost, when he went to the episcopal residence to receive an answer from the auxiliary bishop, to whom he had a few days earlier submitted everything pertaining to the proposed project, he quite unexpectedly encountered the Archbishop himself, Marie-Dominique Sibour. This was a momentous, indeed providential meeting, that not only changed the course of his life but also reshaped his perception of what God was calling him to realize. In response to the Archbishop's flat refusal to approve what he understood as yet another purely contemplative initiative, Eymard hastened to clarify that the scope of the work would be not only adoration, but also to prepare adults for First Communion. Since this kind of pastoral care was lacking, the Archbishop was instantly won over and enthusiastically welcomed Father Eymard.[82]

This work of preparing people for the Lord's Table of Communion would hold a priority for Father Eymard. Mentioning how impressed he was by a similar apostolate being carried out by the Abbé Chevrier, with whom he had spent a whole day in Lyons, he wrote to convince his first companion, Father Raymond de Cuers, that "A purely contemplative life cannot be fully Eucharistic: the hearth has a flame."[83] In fact, from his earliest days as a diocesan priest and later as a Marist, Father Eymard had zealously attended to this important part of his ministry. After 1858, when the community moved to the Faubourg Saint-Jacques, an impoverished working class sector of the city, he gathered the urchins of Paris, whose instruction he saw to personally on many occasions or entrusted either to the members of the community or to well-prepared catechists. August 15, 1859 was the first occasion when twelve lads celebrated their First Communion. He envisaged the expansion of "this beautiful work" to "four or eight centers in Paris," a city that, because some people weren't even christened, was mission territory like "China, Oceania and Africa."[84] He was often called to preach at these occasions, which had a particularly festive joyous character, which is clear in the tone of his sermons based on a text liturgically used for Easter: "This is the day the Lord has made! Let us rejoice and be glad" (Ps 117:24).[85] To publicize this work he wrote two articles about it in a periodical that he had started.[86] A development may be observed in his approach to the preparation for Holy Communion insofar as he sought to lead communicants to discover an intimacy with Christ in the Eucharistic Mystery.[87] This work of predilection progressed in an organized manner through involving lay associates of the Blessed Sacrament.[88]

His heartfelt endeavors in responding to people's deepest spiritual welfare in this regard can be especially seen as a prophetic contribution to paving the way toward the Church's eventual encouragement about giving children access to Holy Communion and frequent, even daily reception of this Sacrament.[89] He advised people never to neglect, out of a sense of unworthiness, dryness or weakness, to heed the Lord's kind invitation to approach the Holy Table at the family feast where they take their place that God reserves especially for his children.[90] Furthermore, his mission in those days, heavily marked by the specter of Jansenism, prophetically pointed to fostering what the Second Vatican Council would later urge, namely, fruitful participation in the divine liturgy, which is most fully realized in sacramental Communion.[91] Nothing better than this expresses the hope-giving ultimate purpose of the Paschal dynamism of the Eucharistic Mystery, which leads people towards

union with the Risen Lord and with one another in the eternal life of
the Holy Trinity. In words recalling the rich teaching of the Fathers
of the Church, he exhorted communicants in one of his sermons at a
First Communion celebration to be most deeply grateful to the Lord
for making them truly "Christophers" and "other Christs," in virtue
of becoming united with Christ and formed into him (cf. Gal 2:20;
4:19). He states that this Sacrament deifies them in a manner not
realized by the other sacraments. Furthermore, he points out here
that the Eucharist is not only the Memorial of the Lord Jesus' death
(1 Cor 11:26), but also the "principle of our glorious resurrection."[92]
It is noteworthy that Eymard uses the phrase "another Christ" (*alter
christus*) as referring to Christians in the original sense it was used
by St. Gregory of Nyssa,[93] although he was also quite well aware that
this expression is applied to priests.[94]

Dispenser of the mysteries of God

In genuine pastoral and fraternal charity Father Eymard's compassionate concern was turned towards the situation of the secular
clergy, many of whom were suffering from isolation and lack of support. He highlighted the importance of caring for priests' spiritual
needs as one of his Congregation's principal apostolic works.[95] His
high regard for the apostolic ministry is similar to that of St. Jean-
Marie Vianney, who said: "The priesthood is the love of the heart of
Jesus."[96] In his correspondence with one of his spiritual daughters,
Virginie Danion, he frankly expressed his dismay about how often
priests show little interest in Eucharistic worship and fear the Eucharistic vocation; he states that in response to this she should become
consumed in her prayer of adoration "for all these cowardly men."[97]
A few months earlier, during his long retreat in Rome he meditated
on the lamentable fact that the wonderful reality of God's love shown
in the mystery of the Incarnation was barely known, thought about,
or preached even by priests.[98]

In notes jotted down for a retreat he dealt with the topic of working out salvation in fear and trembling (cf. Ph 2:12; Mt 10:28), referring to St. John Chrysostom's severe sentence concerning the number of priests who will be damned.[99] He recognized clearly how priests can lose their love for the Eucharist and yield to the great danger of becoming discouraged and lukewarm through the pressing demands of administrative tasks, which drain them of their physical and spiritual energies by routine.[100] Because of this Eymard directed much of his attention to building up their morale and kindling their zeal. He responded to requests of bishops to give retreats to the clergy or seminarians, counseled many, received some into the community for retreats or an opportunity to rest.[101] His realistic solicitude for priests extended most widely insofar as he sought to express a vision about priests coming together to share prayer as well as discussion about their pastoral responsibilities and personal concerns in fraternal friendship. He is reported as saying: "I would leave everything for priests."[102]

The whole apostolically dynamic ministry of the Word and the Sacrament, as Father Eymard perceived it, should impel priests to undertake their task with a missionary zeal to save, sanctify and, indeed, "divinize" people (cf. 2 P 1:4).[103] He pointed out that in proclaiming the words "This is my Body" they call down Christ's presence and set ablaze a furnace in hearts with divine love.[104] He rather trenchantly remarked in his last sermon for the Feast of Pentecost, that instead of proclaiming the abundant life the Lord Jesus announced and bestowed (cf. Jn 10:10), many priests were sadly "caught up in the cult of death."[105] Much earlier he had asked Marguerite Guillot to pray for the kind of men needed for a new congregation: "priests of fire."[106] Such as these, as the Apostle Paul says, are "servants of Christ and dispensers of the mysteries of God" (1 Cor 4:1), words that he quoted often regarding the sacred ministry.[107]

Revolution of love

Father Eymard strenuously combated the fear in people to approach Jesus Christ's table of Holy Communion – a fear inculcated in them by the above recalled soul-damaging errors of the prevalent teachings of Jansenism. This zealous pastor incessantly taught the Johannine doctrine that perfect love casts out fear (cf. 1 Jn 4:18). For him this quality of love is discovered uniquely through the Holy Eucharist, where the Risen Lord reveals himself as humankind's consolation, healer, friend, brother. Neglect of this divinely bestowed means of hope and health-giving salvation, he insisted, was the root cause of the "malaise" of the century, its indifferentism and coldness of heart, desiccation of a sense of apostolate and mission.[108] Later on, in his great Roman retreat, he reflected about how his Congregation would form a "Eucharistic Militia" whose mission is "the most beautiful and most timely" insofar as its task is not so much to defend a truth of faith, "but to combat the great heresy of the century, indifference, to melt the ice hardening all hearts." He perceived that this mission would be realized by apostles who are adorers of the Holy Eucharist.[109] His use of the word "militia"[110] indicates his ardor to engage others in waging spiritual warfare for the sake of promoting the Lord's cause of love, in which his soldiers share the joy of joining the Church triumphant of the saints in heaven, the definitive focus of human hope. This language, particularly typical of spiritual writing of his times, has a long tradition traceable to the age of the martyrs, who are commemorated in the *Te Deum* as "the white-robed army who shed their blood for Christ" (cf. Rv 7:9). Although this language is unattractive to today's mentality, it is nevertheless offset by much else in his teaching that is more inspiring and movingly beautiful throughout his ministry of extensive preaching, counseling and spiritual direction of many people, especially women, or letter-writing. His rich poetic use of imagery is drawn from the Scriptures and also from his being sensitively attuned to the beauty of God's creation.

With the creativity of Christian imagination Eymard's use of imagery of Christ's reign was linked to the biblical theme of God's glory, dear to him.[111] In urging the importance of restoring Christ's social reign, he saw that without this there could be no genuine renewal of humankind. This idea of restoring Christ's reign of love in people's hearts is the overall objective presented in the drafts of the Constitutions of the Congregation that he worked on until his death. It is implied in the abbreviation of the phrase of the Lord's Prayer at the heading of many of his letters: 'A.R.T.' (*Adveniat Regnum Tuum* – "Thy Kingdom Come"). He presented the notion of establishing Christ's kingdom symbolically by means of the solemn cult of exposition of the Blessed Sacrament, before which adorers were as it were courtiers of the Eucharistic Christ on a throne, behind which was draped a royal ermine mantle surmounted by a crown. Although now hardly appropriate, this baroque style of devotion must be understood as pertaining to the pious sensibilities of Eymard's times, in which zealous persons sought to combat the post-Concordat environment of growing secularism in France by asserting a religious triumphalism regarding the nature of the Church, which was identified with God's kingdom instead of being understood as its sacrament and humble servant.[112] Nevertheless, as will be discussed below in dealing with what he discovered during the heart-searching revision of his life in his great Roman retreat, Eymard perceived that Christ's reign, rather than being an external manifestation of pomp and ceremony, must come about within the human heart transformed by the lordship of the Savior's love. He noted that "the royal truth" par excellence is "the Cenacle in me, and glorifying God through me, which God prefers to all the acts of external homage I might perform."[113]

A certain resemblance may be interestingly observed between Eymard's approach and that taken by Charles Wesley (1707-88). Like the evangelical preacher he likewise fostered an affective faith-response to the vibrant call of the Gospel message. It pertains to what has been called a "theology of the heart."[114] Thus, for instance, Father Eymard spoke about the need for experiencing real intimacy with Jesus through love, as John did during the Last Supper:

Love without feeling (*sympathie*) is a laborious virtue, although sometimes sublime, but it doesn't know love's charming aspect or its goodness.... This sweetens the

sacrifices entailed and ensures constancy.... A Christian
needs to experience the proof, the witness of God's personal love. Now it is above all through the Holy Eucharist
that our Lord gives us this so gently that he allows us to
repose a little on his heart like the beloved disciple [cf.
Jn 13:25], to savor at least briefly the sweetness of this
heavenly manna.[115]

The reference here to "heavenly manna" (cf. Rv 2:17) alludes
also to Jesus' promise of giving himself as "the bread from heaven"
(cf. Jn 6:41), the new "manna" that he explained to the bewildered
Jews would surpass and amply fulfill the significance of the food
for the Israelites in their desert wandering and journey toward the
promised land (cf. Jn 6:43ff.). Also implied here is Father Eymard's
insight into the experiential link between the Eucharist and heaven,
its foretaste and incentive to hope since this sacrament both nour-
ishes and strengthens human beings as "the pledge of future glory"
(*pignus futurae gloriae*).[116] He perceived that this sacrament offers
realistic hope to people, since it integrated and transformed them
thoroughly in all dimensions of their being: intellectual, moral and
spiritual.[117] Eymard, in other words, would insist on the intrinsic and
inseparable relation between life and liturgy, contemplation and action, work and worship, which are all gathered into and symbolized
by offering the bread and wine, the fruits of the earth and the work
of human hands.

A keen awareness of the vitalizing quality of God's word led
him to realize the need to bring about a completely new approach to
proclaiming the Gospel of Jesus Christ. His own manner of preaching attracted people. It offered them hope by fostering in them the
possibility of experiencing the delight of paradise which, as he
pointed out on various occasions, is already opened to humankind
in the Eucharistic Banquet. He proclaimed this "good news" from
early preaching to the end of his life.[118] This contrasted sharply to
the tone and message of many a preacher – a tone that was harsh, a

message that was moralistic, reparation-oriented, sin-preoccupied, lacking in inspiration. Instead of being heralds of Christ, the Good News and Light of the world, priests often showed merely the severity of God as Judge, rather than his benign merciful love made manifest through the whole sacramental economy of salvation, especially in the Eucharistic Mystery, wherein is revealed and communicated the strongest preventative against sin and the richest source of joy. He is reported as having remarked:

> We must, you see, start a revolution in the pulpit. We are making a revolution in piety already. When God gives one an idea, as he has given me on this matter, it is not to keep it secret. Today we do not preach our Lord; we do not even mention his holy name. We must preach him, we must nourish the faithful. The present practice tends to purge them until they bleed. Ever since Bossuet all preachers have been negative. It is easy to be carried away, to thunder in the pulpit, but we should feed the faithful.[119]

Quite the opposite of a moralistic kill-joy approach, Eymard's endeavor consisted in raising people's sights above and beyond being focused on themselves and their miserable condition. He led them to recognize that by responding to the revelation of the nearness of God's transcendent grace and truth in the Mystery of Faith they would discover the real joy of living their true worth and ultimate fulfillment as persons according to God's design. In this regard, one recalls the sage advice given by Georges Bernanos' character the Curé Torcy – advice which Father Eymard would certainly have wholeheartedly endorsed:

> A Christian people doesn't mean a lot of little goody-goodies. The Church has plenty of stamina, and isn't afraid of sin. On the contrary, she can look it in the face calmly and even take it upon herself, assume it at times, as Our Lord did.... God has entrusted the Church to keep

that soul alive, to safeguard our candor and freshness.... Christianity alone can exalt it, can raise it to man's own height, to the peak of his dreams.... Joy is in the gift of the Church, whatever joy is possible for this sad world to share.[120]

Father Eymard's sermons emphasized the delight springing from the sense of wonderment, which Pope John Paul II points out,[121] in experiencing Christ's love through the precious gift of the Real Presence. He came to be known as "the priest of the Eucharist" because his constant Eucharistic orientation in preaching and pastoral guidance were rooted in and nourished by his own encounter with the Lord in the prayer of adoration.

Being a man of deep prayer, Eymard taught that here in this encounter in adoration, second only to Holy Communion, was found the wellspring of joy and a foretaste of paradise insofar as adoration of God is the sole delightful occupation of the saints in heaven.[122] He recommended adoration of and visits to the Blessed Sacrament to be made as spiritual communion,[123] which encompassed the essence of what sacramental Communion entails: the experience of yearning for spiritual union with the Lord Jesus – *Maran atha*. The longing, "the language of the heart," becomes fired in contemplation, which he distinguished from meditation, for it draws a person into the inner sanctuary of that reciprocal loving exchange between God and a person mystically described in the Canticle of Canticles: "My beloved is mine and I am his" (Sg 2:16).[124] In the annual retreat he gave to his religious in Paris a year before his death he said: "I maintain as a principle that the grace of the Society is a grace of prayer and that we must be distinguished by that from other religious bodies. This grace is our foundation; naturally as by instinct you must possess the spirit of prayer."[125]

He came to see that it was inadequate to focus only on the reparatory aspect of prayer, as practiced by some groups exclusively dedicated to this. He taught his religious as well as devout members of the faithful a method of prayer that linked adoration of the Blessed

Sacrament intrinsically with the Sacrifice of the Mass – that method of the "Four Ends: adoration, thanksgiving, reparation and petition."[126] He expressed this breakthrough in his thought in the following words about the wide scope of his Congregation's commitment to the far-reaching aspects of a Eucharistic apostolate:

> The end that we are proposing for our little society is to honor Our Lord Jesus Christ in the most Holy Sacrament by the four ends of sacrifice: adoration, thanksgiving, reparation and supplication, or a perpetual mission of prayer. We take the whole of the Holy Sacrament. We… want not only to adore, serve, love Jesus-Eucharistic, but above all to make him known, adored, served and loved by all hearts.[127]

The pasture is thy word[128]

Father Eymard's approach to preaching was based solidly on praying the word of God. This may be seen as flowing from his practice of meditating constantly on the Holy Scriptures, similar to the ancient tradition called *lectio divina*, although he does not use this terminology as such.[129] His sermons or spiritual instructions abundantly show that he was first of all, like the Virgin Mary, a listener to the Lord, whose word resounded in his heart before being proclaimed. Witnesses attested to his spending of hours before the tabernacle in the church, where he carefully prepared himself for his ministry of preaching.[130] He grasped as a young priest the intrinsic complementary connection between the liturgy of the Word and the Eucharistic liturgy. The following words were written when he was a curate at Chatte:

> Look, brethren, how Jesus Christ has fulfilled his promise. We have it entire and in all his deeds as Savior. In the pulpit of truth he proclaims his laws, and on the altar he seals them by his blood. There Jesus Christ becomes

adored in the truth of his body; here he is recognized in the truth of his teaching. From the one and the other of these two tables, Jesus Christ distributes to his children a divine nourishment: on the altar through the Holy Spirit's power and the mystic words,[131] which mustn't be at all considered without trembling, the substance of bread and wine become transformed into the body of our Lord Jesus Christ; here by the same Spirit and the power of the same divine word, Jesus Christ's faithful must be secretly transformed to become his body and his members. This is how Jesus Christ is constituted our truth and our life, so that he may be our unique way. *Ego sum via, veritas et vita* (Jn 14:6).[132]

These sentences harmonize perfectly with the teaching of the Second Vatican Council regarding the importance of the liturgy of the Word as well as the role of the Holy Spirit throughout the Eucharistic celebration and especially the prayer of epiclesis;[133] they recall the doctrine of the Fathers of the Church, who taught that God's holy Word and Sacrament are deserving of the same reverence.[134] He certainly derived this imagery of the "two tables" from that classic from the *devotio moderna*, the *Imitation of Christ*, a source of spirituality to which he had frequent recourse.[135]

His style as a preacher must certainly have been engaging, for, although without the oratorical flourish in vogue among some preachers of his day, witnesses recalled that he was most inspiring to those who listened to him. He learnt the art of communicating, building on the natural gifts of warmth, sincerity and convinced faith he had received abundantly from God.[136] In the context of prayerfully meditating the divine Word and contemplating its continuity in the Eucharistic Mystery, he practiced this art in order to teach people how to use the alphabet of God's language in their lives of faith, hope, love, for, as the Anglican priest-poet George Herbert put it: "Thy Word is all, if we could spell."[137]

The imagery of spreading the Eucharistic "fire" to the four corners of the earth

As shown in many instances, one of Eymard's favorite images for the Eucharist was that of fire in the hearth. He often quotes or refers to St. John Chrysostom's phrase in this regard: "The Eucharist is a burning coal that ignites us."[138] This patristic citation is frequently linked with Jesus' words encapsulating his ardent desire: "I came to cast fire upon the earth; and would that it were already kindled" (Lk 12:49). Indicating the apostolic thrust flowing from contemplative adoration, he often cites this text of the Gospel in sections of various drafts of the Constitutions that deal with the Eucharistic end and means of the Congregation he founded as well as the focus of the ministry of preaching. In his attempt to draw up a rule of life for members of the lay association of the Congregation (the Aggregation of the Blessed Sacrament), this Lucan verse is a key to emphasizing the primacy of divine dynamism of love in their Eucharist-centered lives. It was through Father Eymard's inspiration and endeavors to enkindle this fire of the immense love of the Lord's gift in the Eucharistic Mystery that after his death there resulted various developments on a worldwide ecclesial scale: International Eucharistic Congresses,[139] the Priests' Eucharistic League,[140] the movement for frequent Communion and the First Communion of children.[141]

Even before the foundation of the Congregation of the Blessed Sacrament, Father Eymard often preached on how the fire of divine grace in the Eucharist enables people to be generous and kind, especially in the pardoning of others in virtue of being reconciled by the Blood of the world's Savior. In an outline of a sermon, in which he referred to the same Lucan verse and also quotes Chrysostom's phrase, he answers his rhetorical questions: "What is this fire? Where is it found? It is the fire of love. The Eucharist is its center."[142] In another sermon, again quoting the same texts, he specified that divine love manifested by the Eucharist has three properties similar to fire: it gives light, warms and generates life.[143] Elsewhere, in preaching to

First Communicants he compared the Eucharistic fire to the inextinguishable burning bush that symbolizes the reality of the consuming fire of God who is love (cf. Dt 4:24; Heb 12:29; 1 Jn 4:8, 16).[144] Writing to a member of the Third Order of Mary from the Marist college of La Seyne-sur-Mer (near Toulon), where he was the superior, he expressed delight that her idea of domestic adoration received the approval of the Cardinal Archbishop of Lyons, for he saw in this a way of torching the indifference in France and Europe:

> I find that one is too far from the Holy Eucharist, that one doesn't preach often enough on this mystery of love par excellence; so souls suffer, they become entirely sensual and materialistic in their piety, clinging to creatures in a disordered way, because they don't know how to find their consolation and strength in our Lord.... Remember that when one has placed a Eucharistic spark in someone's heart, a divine seed of life and all the virtues become implanted in the heart; that's enough so to speak for this person.[145]

It was undoubtedly this seed, this spark, of Eucharistic love that he sowed in the soul of Julian Tenison Woods, an Englishman who stayed for a little while at the college of La Seyne and received from Father Eymard spiritual direction that guided him in discerning his vocation, a vocation that took him to Australia. There, after his ordination to the ministerial priesthood in Adelaide he co-founded with St. Mary MacKillop the Sisters of St. Joseph of the Sacred Heart and also later on the Sisters of Perpetual Adoration in Brisbane. Tenison Woods wrote his recollection of Father Eymard:

> Of all the different people I have met with in life he is one who has left the deepest impression on my mind. He certainly was a saint, with the sweetest patience in all his dealings with the members of the College, both boys and professors. He was a man also of the deepest spiritual knowledge with a recollection and spirit of piety which shone in all his actions. He was a tall thin man with a face

and expression of an Angel.... He... helped me more even than Dr. Faber or anyone of my spiritual directors.... Father Eymard was in my mind a great saint in his own way as Dr. Faber, but differing completely from him. He was shy and retiring with a hidden deep devotion: a spiritual life with the spirit of the Blessed Eucharist, for the honor and perpetual adoration of which he founded his Order.[146]

There is also another image that Father Eymard had recourse to in bringing out the educative aspect of the Eucharist, which he compares to the role of a mother, as for instance in these touching words in an address to a group of women:

When a mother wishes to teach her child to walk, she goes before him/her, holds out her arms and as the child approaches the mother goes back a step and so on until the child has become confident to walk without being held. Jesus in a similar way treats a soul he loves.[147]

After this he pointed out that the essence of the Christian life is discovered in the Lord's tender manner of nourishing his followers on Eucharistic love:

Here is the true starting point of holiness, of perfection. I'm talking about Eucharistic love because to know how to love one must have been loved, nourished on a mother's milk, through receiving communion – *ad ubera portabimini* [Is 66:12]; to be *devout*, one must be embraced by Eucharistic love, to have received this sacred fire, this divine energizing power (like the confessors and martyrs); St. John Chrysostom said: *Carbo est* [Eucharistia].[148]

As St. Augustine had stated, Father Eymard encouraged people, and especially his religious, to emulate the attitude of the Beloved Disciple, John, who leaning on the Master's bosom drank in the divine secrets of eternal life (cf. Jn 13:23).[149] For him this attitude opens the way to an experiential awareness of the astonishing truth of the bounteous love of Christ. This "maternal" imagery recalls the use of it by the Fathers and mystics, who thereby communicated their understanding of divine tenderness and their familiarity with the Savior's loving kindness.[150]

The imagery of fire and motherly feeding – among others as well – highlighted for Eymard what was of paramount importance and centrality regarding the truth of God's supreme gift of love communicated by the Lord Jesus in the Eucharist. Unto the very end of his life he ceaselessly and unwearyingly proclaimed this essential truth, which he considered as the climactic act of divine Revelation, to which the Church points as John the Baptist did: "Behold the Lamb of God."[151] Thus, in his series of Thursday evening instructions given in the chapel at Paris he commented on Jesus' promise of the Bread of Life (Jn 6). The words of his very last instruction on July 16, 1868, before going to La Mure where he died, merit recalling at some length, since they are his adieu, his lasting testimony to the truth of divine love, that truth conveyed not by books or teachers, but only by the Lord himself in faith's life-giving form of nourishment in the Eucharistic Mystery:

> One doesn't come to the Eucharist by reason; whoever has wanted to apply reason is sunk in the ocean of God's power, and can't do this without denigrating our Lord, [without] setting oneself up as a judge. Nor must one even stare…. [T]his is to insult, yet, you still want to look at our Lord! If your eyes were to meet they would melt…. Thomas had raised the objection of the people at Capernaum, who wanted to see to believe…. If our Lord comes under a visible aspect, he does this not to give us faith, but to stimulate piety, wonderment, love – this wouldn't be faith, since one already has faith. It is to console, expand the heart, not to bestow faith, for faith doesn't rely on the

evidence of the senses; religion has miracles. But the Eucharist rests on divine veracity – hence, one doesn't come to it by sense knowledge, miracles – by divine veracity alone. The Eucharist was given in a form of food. The soul must above all be nourished by it. So remember clearly that it is spiritual food.… Go to communion for strength, not for feelings, not for temporal but for eternal life.[152]

What Father Eymard realized and passionately yearned to convey may be compared to the philosopher Pascal's famous words about the heart having its reasons that are inaccessible to reason.[153] This presentation of the "logic" of divine love also echoes St. Augustine's teaching about how God sets ablaze, strengthens and expands the capacity of the human heart by etching into it the hope to abide eternally in the delightful presence of his love.[154]

Throughout his preaching or instructions he carefully developed themes that he always related and wove into the magnificent tapestry of God's love lavishly communicated in the Eucharistic Mystery. He delighted to meditate, reflect, and contemplate the variegated facets of the Eucharist, that "many-splendored thing."[155] This was the starting point, center and goal of all his preaching and teaching, as it became increasingly and profoundly the leitmotif of his whole life. In an original approach, which sprang from his Spirit-guided personal experience and penetration into the depths of this mystery, he didn't just repeat traditional Catholic teaching in a dry, abstract textbook-like fashion, but presented the Mystery of Faith in a refreshingly attractive way, so that it may be said without exaggeration that his words may be compared to those of Jesus as quickened with "spirit and life" (cf. Jn 6:63). His words, filled with references to or quotations from the Holy Scriptures, have an immediacy of appeal like Jesus' "parables of sun light."[156] This appeal to the imagination effectively touched and moved all who listened to him, awakening them to respond from the core of their being, that is, the divine image and likeness impressed into them.

Eymard could be said to be a poet of the soul's Bread.[157]This is true not merely because of his fine sensitivity and gifted capacity to employ words with artistry. His words expressed not merely thoughts *about* God and, particularly *about* the Eucharist; rather, he excelled in living the vocation pertaining particularly to the intrinsic quality of a priest, namely, to proclaim the most original, most exciting and ultimately daring statement that renders present and manifests the Lord Jesus' communication of himself, in virtue of which God becomes handed over to humankind.[158] The words of Eymard the priest didn't only superbly handle the mysteries of faith with reverence as befits their sacredness. His words embodied, so to speak, his dominant realization of the divine Word made Sacrament. They spelled out, or rather, communicated the abundant life springing from the Risen Lord's "eucharisted gifts,"[159] in which the divine Word fulfils all human yearnings, sharpening them into authentic hope, focusing and orienting humankind toward grasping God's loving design and culminating appointed purpose: communication and being-in-communion.

Pathway to the Cenacle

Like many of the greatest teachers of the spiritual journey into God, Father Eymard wrestled with those aspects of human experience that brought about diversion and division in him and impeded his complete conversion, integration and union with God. He had indeed long ago seen his need of recollection and simplicity, reproving himself in various notes of personal retreats. During his nine-week long retreat at Rome in 1865, however, he was most self-critical. This retreat, begun on January 25, 1865 – the Feast of the Conversion of St. Paul – was undertaken while he awaited the decision of the Roman Curia about obtaining the Cenacle in Jerusalem to set up a center of Eucharistic Adoration.[160] Although the decision turned out to be contrary to his plans, his sojourn in Rome brought him to a turning point in his whole approach to religious life, to understanding the deepest significance of a Eucharist-centered vocation and its implications regarding the renewal of Christian spirituality rooted in the Paschal Mystery. Appropriately his image in describing his struggle to follow his vocation was Jacob: "I have been very much like Jacob, always en route."[161]

He profited from his prolonged stay in Rome to scrutinize his natural impulses, chastising himself about his motivations, lack of discipline and seriousness, which dissipated, disoriented and sapped his mental and spiritual energies, while easily making him a prey to activism that was leading him away from being genuinely apostolic. He summarized the obstacles to his spiritual life as consisting principally in his natural pride and vanity, because of which he recognized his ingratitude to the Lord. He saw that the way to discover afresh the deep meaning of his calling lay in devoting himself more to interiority fostered by recollection and a recovery of childlike simplicity, rather than in placing emphasis on exterior acts in serving God and becoming preoccupied about the external trappings of Eucharistic cult. He insightfully perceived also that a duty-fixated mentality was insufficient and unworthy of God who desires the human heart above all, not what a person does or sets himself to achieve through a preconceived notion of moral perfectionism that operates in an attitude of rigorous voluntarism. He became lucidly aware that such an approach only promotes arrogance and conceited self-complacency when being successful, or discouragement and abandonment of hope when failing to achieve self-set goals. He reproved in himself this mindset as pertaining to the kind of service given by a mercenary or by one driven by fear rather than by the dynamic free impulse of love in response to the presence of Christ's ultimate gift of himself in the Sacrament par excellence of love. He resolved to take the necessary steps toward making an appropriate response to this great gift, steps requiring becoming more recollected (gathered) in Christ. He grasped that conversion of heart comes about through entering deeply into constant conversation with him, for in this manner one discovers what St. Paul meant about having in oneself "the mind of Christ" (cf. Phil 2:5), which requires being open to the transforming grace of the Holy Spirit, who leads towards overcoming the limiting tendency of egoism and reveals the divine image and likeness. His experience during this retreat enabled him thus to deepen his perspective and purpose regarding what the Lord had been orienting him towards from his baptism.[162]

His weeks on retreat in Rome had enabled Father Eymard to arrive at a crucial watershed that entailed taking this decisive stand, one that was an entirely Spirit-inspired and grace-sustained deeper conversion of heart. It may be said that this retreat was a paschal experience; it was his "passover" to actualize existentially the Apostle's words, to which he referred or quoted more than any other text of Holy Scripture: "It is no longer I who live, but Christ who lives in me; and the life I now live in the flesh I live by faith in the Son of God" (Gal 2:20).[163]

His conversion to realize this in himself may be considered as fitting into what is called a "midlife crisis" leading to a "second journey" or "second conversion" as illustrated in the complex patterns and processes of the woof and weave of many persons' fascinating stories of coming to Christ: for example, of Paul, Augustine, Ignatius of Loyola, Teresa of Avila, Wesley, Newman, Dorothy Day and Mother Teresa of Calcutta.[164] Up to this point Eymard had not at all been living in a frivolous way; nevertheless, during the graced experience of the prolonged retreat his awareness was so sharpened as to recognize his need for a greater, total dedication to fulfill the Lord's calling him to live and make known the depth of being in communion with God through the Eucharistic Mystery.

Eymard's realization during this retreat had brought him to the kind of awareness that the poet T.S. Eliot describes as "the intersection of the timeless moment":

> The end of all our exploring
> Will be to arrive where we started

> And know the place for the first time...
> A condition of complete simplicity
> (Costing not less than everything)...[165]

The cost was the complete surrender of himself during his thanksgiving after celebrating the Eucharist in making the vow of personality near the end of his Roman retreat of 1865.[166] Various spiritual authors no doubt had an influence on Eymard's decision to make this vow.[167] It was the climactic point to which his journey had led, a point, however, that must be seen in relation to his frequently repeated teaching on the gift of self modeled on Christ's total self-giving in the Eucharist. His contribution to spirituality in this regard is most significant insofar as it refines the doctrine of Christian perfection as taught from the time of the Fathers,[168] by situating the scope of Christian perfection not only in relation to Gospel values, but in the light of the Lord's inestimable gift at the heart of the Church, namely, the Paschal Mystery celebrated in the Eucharist.[169] The significance of this vow is quite different in scope to the vow of greater perfection that St. Teresa of Avila made in 1560, that is, to choose and do always what is most perfect in order to be of better service in guiding others in living the gospel and prayer.[170] For Eymard this step in making such a vow meant not merely taking decisions to act in a way one perceived to be more pleasing to God, but the complete surrender of his self so that Christ lives and acts in and through him, as St. Paul put it (Gal 2:19-20).

Quoting this text of the Apostle, he carefully explained to his brethren and to the Sister Servants the meaning of the vow of personality as the radical surrender not merely of things one has or does, but of one's very self, one's entire being. "Look, you are Servants," he told the Sisters at Nemours. "This is your name; and what is a servant? It's a person who has made a voluntary gift of service.... Don't work for yourselves, kill your human personality from Adam and replace it by Our Lord and say: *It is no longer I who live...* Here's what serving Our Lord in religious life is."[171] In giving priority to Christ's being in him rather than to offering to him things one has or what one does, Peter-Julian goes to the root of Jesus' repeated paradoxical challenge about losing one's life to save it (cf. e.g., Lk 9:24; Jn 12:25). This insight clearly implies even greater depths than what is stated in C.S. Lewis' words quoted at the beginning of this chapter: "It is when I turn to Christ, when I give myself up to His Personality, that I first begin to have a real personality of my own." But, Peter-Julian's vow of personality requires not being focused on or concerned in the slightest about one's self or one's own importance. This entails entering fully into the existential dynamism of Jesus' paschal exodus (cf. Lk 9:31).[172] Eymard emphasized that such complete commitment could be made only because of being led and sustained by the inspiration of the Holy Spirit and undertaken in virtue of divine grace. He pointed out that only a few saints had practiced it, while nevertheless recommending it as particularly appropriate for members in his Congregations who felt called to make this vow.[173] The underlying gist of Eymard's teaching was to awaken a constant, interior, intense, complete and lively sense of intimate communion with the divine presence.[174]

His great retreat in 1865 enabled him to rethink radically what should be the characteristic virtue of an adorer, which he saw should be consistent with Christ's attitude in the Eucharistic Sacrament, namely, a self-emptying in the humility of love, rather than the virtue of religion, as was his formerly held view.[175] This discovery is reflected in his words during the last annual retreat he preached to his religious when he insisted that love should be above all the motivation in everything:

> A person who mortifies himself because of justice obtains peace. One who does this out of love is filled with joy. Look at the Curé d'Ars. Here is a sure sign of God's love. Mortification because of justice doesn't prove that one loves God more than oneself. One can carry out all that is commanded and be interiorly very peevish. Mortification of the spirit goes straight to God.... It doesn't desire anything but only God for his own sake and never asks from

him anything for the self. Ah! What a way to approach God! If I had only understood this fifteen years ago! But I have understood it too late. This is a treasure I'm handing over to you. Know how to profit by it.[176]

More clearly than he had previously seen, during his long retreat in Rome Eymard discovered that the school of perfection, where a person learns how to live the gift of self perfectly, is the "interior cenacle."[177] This discovery was indeed immensely more important and worthwhile than his cherished project about acquiring the Cenacle at Jerusalem.[178] For he came to appreciate that in the divine milieu of the interior cenacle a person's whole life becomes focused on the truth of Jesus' self-gift of love in the Eucharist and thus becomes oriented toward the transcendent dimension for which human beings are created. By entering into the interior cenacle a person is enabled to experience "the logic of unconditional gift… an economy of gratuitousness."[179] As Father Eymard told the Sister Servants, this entails an "interior education" that "consists in learning to think, speak and converse with our Lord."[180] This is nothing other than being drawn in the dynamism of responding to God joyously and freely by a life of thanksgiving and praise for his gracious generosity. The condition for total commitment, Father Eymard would emphasize to his brethren, requires a deeper quality in living that involves recollecting one's memory and imagination.[181] The only solution he saw and proposed for society "dying because it has lost its center of truth and charity" was for people to become raised up from their experience of isolation and spiritual desolation and enlivened again through Eucharistic adoration around "our Emmanuel" who alone unites them.[182]

Recollection – the art of Christian discipleship in becoming Eucharist-hearted

The significance of recollection for Father Eymard is above all that of a being gathered in God. It prepares the way forward to realizing the hope of reaching the transcendent vocation to which every person is called. Through it a person becomes single-minded and wholly converged on Christ, who is both the divine model as well as the interior teacher leading human beings by his Spirit to praise God's magnificent munificence. Thus, he pointed out in the spiritual guidelines he wrote for the lay association of the Blessed Sacrament:

> Love! Behold the starting point of the Christian life. This is God's outreach to his creature, Jesus Christ's for humankind. Nothing is more fitting than this for human beings to have towards God. But before being the starting point, Jesus' love should be a rallying point at which all human faculties become focused in recollection – a school where one learns to know Jesus Christ, an academy where one's spirit studies, copies his or her divine model, where the imagination itself discovers love in all the bounty and beauty of its heart and deeds.[183]

Here is the secret of the saint: being recollected or gathered by and into God, who is simply love. It is what Auguste Rodin must have observed in Father Eymard, who guided him during the five months he spent as a novice in the Congregation to understand that his true métier, his vocation, lay in the exacting discipline of being an artist. One of Rodin's aphorisms is of Eymardian inspiration: "The artist must create a spark before he can make a fire, and before art is born, the artist must be ready to be consumed by the fire of his own creation." A fundamental quality of this disciplined life, a lesson he must have acquired from imitating his spiritual master, was that of focusing on and experiencing, somewhat like the Creator-Potter (cf. Gn 2:7; Is 64:8b; Rm 9:21a), a sense of relation with the subject of his artistic endeavor – an endeavor of playing with clay from which he drew out the spirituality of a human being. One of Rodin's early works was none other than a bust of Eymard, whose features and intensity of gaze he finely captured.[184] This piece may be regarded as a study in recollection. The following lines from a poem by Rowan Williams illustrate this sculptor's total engagement in carrying out his task:

> Rodin's fingers: probe, pinch, ease open,
> polish, calm. Keep still, he says,
> *recueille-toi*....[185]

Recollection, as Eymard realized, is much more than a concentration of mind over matter; it is not a flight from the world nor the kind of classic attitude of a Neo-Platonist philosopher, whose eyes, as in the portraits from antiquity, are intent on the 'inner world' of abstract absolute truth and "flash out at us, revealing an inner life hidden in a charged cloud of flesh."[186] Rather, it entails the deep experience of the life of the Spirit, into which every person is called by the Father to respond freely and faithfully to his Word incarnate, redeeming and recreating this world through love. Recollection crucially important for Eymard meant allowing this Word to resound within a person, awakened spiritually, that is, being-present, being-response to God's presence, the reality of which is focused sacramentally in Christ's giving of himself in the Eucharistic Mystery. His teaching on recollection reaches its apogee in what he said regarding the transformation of a person through Holy Communion.[187] The experience of being recollected, he taught, is integrally a matter of discovering God's loving presence in a sense of intimate communion, which for him is most appropriately symbolized by the imagery of the interior cenacle. In living prayerfully recollected in this atmosphere of the cenacle a person becomes renewed, absorbed and transformed in the dynamic covenantal bond of hope. Recollection as a sense of being present in loving awareness was for him thus both the means to and end of being-in-communion with the Gift of God par excellence which Christ communicates in the Paschal Sacrament of the Eucharist.

Particularly in his last three years Father Eymard's approach to the spiritual life shows a remarkable development as it became more characterized by a childlike spirit of self-surrender to the gentle transforming power of God's gracious design to confirm persons through the Eucharistic Presence of the Risen Lord in their faith-experience of being loved by God, which is the basis and ultimate focus of Christian hope. His attention became more oriented toward teaching the crucial importance of recollection, not so much as demanding an ascetical corrective self-discipline in rigorous vigilance over distracting influences of sense perception, as he had formerly exercised or insisted on, but as that habitual attitude facilitating the proper functioning of the "inner eye," to which the Fathers of the Church and mystics often refer.[188] In pointing to the condition of childlike simplicity he refers to St. Paul's teaching about looking away from ourselves in order to be enabled to perceive with the "enlightened eyes of the heart" (Eph 1:18) and thus come to behold and reflect "the glory of the Lord, being changed into his likeness" (2 Cor 3:18).[189] This in a sense recalls what William Blake wrote:

> This life's five windows of the soul
> Distorts the Heavens from pole to pole,
> And leads you to believe a lie
> When you see with, not thro' the eye.[190]

On various occasions Father Eymard encouraged people to live like the Blessed Virgin Mary and the saints in imitating Jesus' attitude of meekness and humility of heart (Mt 11:29). He pointed to the simplicity of the child that Jesus insisted is the absolute condition for entertaining any hope to enter heaven (cf. Mt 18:3; Jn 3:3). In quoting these texts in many conferences or sermons[191] he said that simplicity must be the "form and basis" of religious life, for without it there is "spiritual decadence," while with it there is found contentment in living out the experience of prayer and its implications.[192] Recollection in his teaching is thus not so much a discipline, as Christian discipleship of remembering or "memorial" (*anamnesis*) of the Lord in an expectation of hope for his coming (cf. 1 Cor 11:24ff.). In this manner recollection is perfected to become Eucharist-hearted, for it leads to an authentically grateful recognition of the form inherent in all features of reality and, above all, it shows the way to a genuine spirit of adoration – that openness to what God graciously reveals, makes manifest and communicates concretely of his mystery of Being-Love proclaimed and celebrated in the Paschal Sacrament of the Eucharist.[193]

One idea, but the field is vast... entirely Eucharistic

A careful sifting through Eymard's teaching reveals the mystery of the man, and moreover, the mystery that captivated and possessed this man's heart. Eymard had a gift for relating to people, a gift that he turned to best effect throughout his priestly ministry. From his earliest years he was certainly drawn to respond to the Real Presence of Christ in the Eucharist. What is clearly evident also is his passion to penetrate to the transformative core significance of the reality of Christ's presence being poured out through the Eucharist. What is particularly inspiring in Eymard is how throughout his life he was impelled to search relentlessly into the depths of this Mystery of Faith and to communicate his passion to know and serve in love the Eucharistic Christ. Certainly he was inevitably conditioned, as every person is, by the cultural and religious climate of his time so that his response to the Eucharistic Mystery was expressed in the post-Tridentine apologetic language and tripartite perspective of Real Presence, Sacrifice, Communion, as well as the devotional and ascetical practices available to him and his contemporaries.

It can be legitimately asked, however, whether this was all. It would be anachronistic to read into his words the theological approach of the Second Vatican Council, to interpret his statements in the light of the fuller, biblical and patristic based teaching of the twentieth century. To what extent, then, can it be claimed that he was "a man before his time," a prophet of the now realized fuller scope of the Paschal Mystery celebrated in the liturgy? What is strikingly noticeable, however, is how he sensitively read the "signs of the times" as pointing to the need for a new approach to the Eucharist. He saw that this approach has to go beyond perceiving the Sacrament as a static reality in order to ensure renewal in the Church, a renewal of Christians' hearts and lives in realizing their missionary vocation to offer hope to a world grown indifferent to the Gospel. In a letter to Madame Natalie Jordan, one of his closest friends and devoted spiritual daughters, he shared his vision of the extensive scope opening up before the little Congregation taking its first steps. After telling her about the realization in Paris of the "beautiful and lovely idea", namely that of setting up perpetual adoration of Jesus Christ in the Eucharist, he hastens to add:

> Love doesn't stop there; it needs zeal, the fire rises up, expands, wants to encompass everything; the religious of the most Blessed Sacrament devote themselves to the Eucharistic ministry – by preaching Forty Hours devotion in parishes, retreats to First Communicants, the work of preparing adults for First Communion, and the association of adoration. Thus you see there is but one idea, but the field is vast, but one that is entirely Eucharistic.[194]

Especially from the time of the coming to birth of the Congregations he founded Eymard perceived that the widest pastoral dimension is integral to the very purpose for which the Savior-Lord provided the gift of himself as the living Bread for the life of the world (cf. Jn 6:51), that is, to sustain people in their pilgrim journey in hope toward the abundance of eternal life (cf. Jn 10:10; 17:3).[195] He was stretched by the leading of the Spirit to grasp that this purpose was beyond what could be imagined, for it pertains to what God reveals in his wisdom (cf. 1 Cor 2:9) as a design to draw even the noblest human sense of perspective and purpose into the paschal ambit of the dynamism of divine hope. His attraction to contemplate God's design of love worked out in the sacramental dispensation of redemption, his delight to adore the Lord Jesus who is received here, as St. Augustine had pointed out[196] – this goaded him to be tireless in encouraging people to allow themselves to believe in love, that is, to be drawn by the Father's gift of the Spirit (cf. Jn 6:44f., 65) into exploring through faith-sustained love how to live from the Eucharist, which, being "the source and summit of the Church's life and mission,"[197] is the wellspring of all holiness and hope.

A progressive development of his insight about serving the Eucharistic Lord with joy is clear throughout Eymard's deepening understanding of this Sacrament as having been instituted to manifest God's love for the world – that love which is compassionate and actively at work. Seeing it as the extension or continuation of the mystery of the redemptive Incarnation, he understood Eucharistic Communion as both the end and also the means of bringing to fulfillment humankind's hope of the transformation and unity reached finally in heaven.[198]

Peter-Julian Eymard learned to be a disciple and apostle of the Eucharist by being an adorer of the mystery of Jesus' gift of self. He became docile in appreciating the fullest scope of Jesus' ministry of compassion for the multitudes. His whole ministry consisted in calling, gathering and inspiring people to realize the transforming communion of the hope springing from the Lord's Paschal Mystery. His teaching on the importance of sacramental communion can be seen as showing that he grasped the essential connection between the celebration of Mass, adoration of the Blessed Sacrament and Christian living, for through each of these the faithful encounter and become more deeply related to Christ and one another.[199] In this he was ahead of his time. He was, thus, a prophet of the Eucharist by pointing people to discover that the fulfillment of their deepest hope consists in worshipping God in spirit and truth. In seeking to make the complete gift of himself generously to God and to others in the Spirit of the Lord Jesus, he shows the joy and worth of being truly human not only as an ideal, but a hope that is possible when lived in a communion of brotherly service in love. This is the fullness of the hope signified by the Eucharistic Mystery.

4

"Heart speaks unto heart"[200]

John Henry Newman

(1801 – 1890)

Seeker of Truth in Communion

Newman's was a voice in the wilderness in the English Catholicism of his day. Some may have realized already that it was a prophetic voice; and we may claim that the Second Vatican Council has proved the fact. *Bishop Christopher Butler O.S.B.*[201]

Not only this Council [Vatican II] but also the present time can be considered in a special way as Newman's hour, in which, with confidence in divine providence, he placed his great hopes and expectations: "Perhaps my name is to be turned to account as a sanction and outset by which others who agree with me in opinion should write and publish instead of me, and thus begin the transmission of views in religious and intellectual matters congenial with my own, to the generation after me." And it is precisely the present moment that suggests, in a particularly pressing and persuasive way, the study and diffusion of Newman's thought. *Pope Paul VI*[202]

The drama of Newman's life invites us to examine our lives, to see them against the vast horizon of God's plan, and to grow in communion with the Church of every time and place: the Church of the apostles, the Church of the martyrs, the Church of the saints, the Church which Newman loved and to whose mission he devoted his entire life.… Newman, by his own account, traced the course of his whole life back to a powerful experience of conversion which he had as a young man.… Newman's life also teaches us that passion for the truth, intellectual honesty, and genuine conversion are costly. *Pope Benedict XVI*[203]

"Surely he was no ordinary man" – these words by which John Henry Newman described Augustine of Hippo may quite aptly be applied to him.[204] Like that great convert of the early Church Newman also was

> A man of affectionate and tender feelings, and open and amiable temper; and, above all, he sought for some excellence external to his own mind, instead of concentrating all his contemplations on himself.[205]

Having a similar loveable and sympathetic disposition to the African Father, Newman would go on to cite at length those sentences in which Augustine relates his anguished state of soul at the death of a dear friend of his youth.[206] In the estimation of both these tender-hearted, highly intelligent men, Augustine and Newman, friendship was one of the finest qualities pertaining to the spiritual excellence of being truly human as well as a sign of sharing the hope of being united in the beatific vision of God's Communion with all the saints.

Newman has also been compared to St. Thomas More,[207] because of many similar personal endowments and qualities: fidelity to conscience, search for truth and also an enormous capacity for friendship.[208] Being a reflective person who cherished solitude, Newman cites St. Philip Neri's rule on humility: *Secretum meum mihi.*[209] This phrase of the Latin Vulgate (cf. Is 24:16) can be paraphrased: my being is mysterious; it belongs to God alone. But he also cultivated friendships particularly with persons "whose faces are turned towards God... for they wait for Christ."[210] Empathy for such persons helped him to penetrate the meaning of prayer, which he described as

> *divine* converse... not indeed thereby meaning converse of words only, but intercourse and manner of living generally.... [P]rayer, I say, has what may be called a *natural* effect, in spiritualizing and elevating the soul. A man is no longer what he was before; gradually, imperceptibly to himself, he has imbibed a new set of ideas, and be-

come imbued with fresh principles.… Such is the power
of God's secret grace acting through those ordinances
which He has enjoined us.… As speech is the organ of
human society, and the means of human civilization, so
is prayer the instrument of divine fellowship and divine
training.[211]

In his view genuine Christian friendships, insofar as they encourage constancy in seeking truth in a communion of love, intensify an uninterrupted desire for God that is hope.[212] For Newman friendship with persons having the "habit of prayer" provided a safeguard against various "faults of mind" that were as common in his day as they are in today's spirit of relativistic subjectivism: an ignorance of and disregard for the necessity of "doctrinal truth"; preference for "caprice and change" and arbitrariness in choosing "a scheme of religion" for oneself; a shiftiness of opinion "going first a little this way, then a little that, according to the loudness and positiveness with which others speak… at the mercy of the last speaker."[213]

He found many likeminded friends at Oxford – Richard Hurrell Froude, who introduced him to love the Blessed Sacrament and the Church's Divine Office; John Keble and Edward Pusey, from whom he learned to appreciate the rich inheritance of the Church's Tradition. He sustained this conversation with those whom he counted as lifelong friends, like William Bowden and Henry Wilberforce. He valued and cultivated friendly exchanges in copious letters with various persons, male and female. He knew the deep solace that the loyalty of friendship provides when his spirits were at low ebb and he experienced a sense of failure because of being misunderstood or unjustifiably the object of others' suspicions or criticism. His influence and example played no small part in leading many persons to conversion, like the Jesuit poet Gerard Manley Hopkins, or when they turned to him for counsel at moments of spiritual crisis. Sir (later Lord) John Acton had also been one of his friends until their differences of approach in regard to some issues, especially the question of papal infallibility, wedged them apart. Acton, however, never forgot his debt of gratitude to Newman, who had stood by him through the years during which he endured virtual exile and opprobrium by the Catholic hierarchy. Acton always admired him for his intellectual perspicacity as "the greatest Roman Catholic to appear in England since the Reformation."[214] Newman for his part was ever genial and courteous towards that great historian, as he was to all. He possessed the qualities of a gentleman that he set out in his famous description of what these entailed: never to inflict pain, to be tolerant and forbearing, while having the good sense not to be affronted by insults, to conduct oneself toward enemies as if they would one day become friends, and to be greatly concerned "to make everyone at their ease and at home";[215] – or simply, in Hopkins' phrase, "mannerly-hearted."[216]

The kernel of Newman's thought about the high value he set on friendship is found in his sermon entitled "Love of Relations and Friends."[217] Here he pointed out that Christian love is not merely a natural virtue, as it was considered by the ancients, nor a matter of philanthropy, but a grace freely given by God who through friendship prepares human beings for his providential work of human redemption or at-onement. In another sermon he says that the deepest respect akin to reverence is due to one's friends without diminishing at all the priority of the worship due to God:

> No one really loves another who does not feel a certain reverence towards him. When friends transgress this sobriety of affection, they may indeed continue associates for a time, but they have broken the bond of union. It is mutual respect which makes friendship lasting.[218]

As the model of friendship, he proposed that of Jesus' love for John, who is "a memorial and pattern (as far as man can be), of love, deep, contemplative, fervent, unruffled, unbounded."[219] Against the notion that "the love of many is superior to the love of one or two" he maintained that friendship for those close to us is "the best preparation for loving the world at large, and loving it duly and wisely."[220]

Newman's appreciation of the company of friends, however, never overshadowed his conviction about the closeness of God's presence, which he recognized as an absolute and ultimately vitalizing need to everyone's innermost personal being. As he put it in a sermon:

> We know that even our nearest friends enter into us but partially, and hold intercourse with us only at times; whereas the consciousness of a perfect and enduring Presence, and it alone, keeps the heart open.[221]

Although the language of the phrases "enter into us" and "hold intercourse with us" in this sentence may seem embarrassing to us today because of their physical and sexual connotation, what Newman is referring to are those rare instances of communion between persons. The profound significance of such experiences cannot, indeed must not, and need not be complicated by prudishness or false moralism; it refers to the reciprocal interlacing – indeed, interpenetration – between the beings of persons related in genuine love. This love in friendship is the gift of the Holy Spirit, who graces and enables human beings to share in the life of the Three Divine Persons' intimacy of relatedness in communion. With a grateful heart Newman saw all human experiences in the perspective of God, who ultimately matters and alone reveals meaning and purpose, design and beauty in the world:

> Life passes, riches fly away, popularity is fickle, the senses decay, the world changes, friends die. One alone is constant; One alone is true to us; One alone can be true; One alone can be all things to us; One alone can supply our needs; One alone can train us up to our full perfection; One alone can give a meaning to our complex and intricate nature; One alone can give us tune and harmony;

One alone can form and possess us. Are we allowed to put ourselves under His guidance? This surely is the only question.[222]

Newman thus kept in focus the doctrine of the "Communion of Saints" – a doctrine that he understood as the basis for people being united truly in the kingdom of God, which is present in the sacramental mystery of the Church.[223] When he became a convert to Rome from the Church of England, the cost was great, as he described in the novel, *Loss and Gain* (1848), the first work he wrote as a Catholic. To many, Newman's loss to the Oxford Movement and, indeed, to the Anglican Church, was regarded as a defection. When recalling the story of his own journey over to Rome, Ronald Knox, the most distinguished convert to Catholicism since John Henry Newman, states that he thought of Newman's conversion in terms of Robert Browning's poem "The Lost Leader."[224] Knox confesses that he himself felt the same pathos Newman expressed in the last sermon he preached at Littlemore.[225] The sermon to which Knox alluded was that on "The Parting of Friends" – preached two years before being received into the Catholic Church on October 9th, 1845,[226] by the saintly Italian missionary Passionist priest to England Dominic Barberi.[227]

Hope for that better country

In his lifelong endeavor to grasp the saving truth of Christ's sacramental mystery, that endeavor which he continued to deepen after he became a Catholic, Newman saw the need to be strengthened by the "light of faith" which enables human beings to participate in the fullness of life in the divine light. He regarded "The visible world… without its divine interpretation" and "Holy Church in her sacraments and her hierarchical appointments… but a symbol of those heavenly facts which fill eternity."[228] His pastoral aim was always to encourage people to penetrate beyond this world's appearances and thus enter the domain of the deeper reality revealed by God. His constant emphasis on this is illustrated clearly in the following:

> There are two worlds, "the visible, and the invisible," as the Creed speaks – the world we see, and the world we do not see.... The world we see we know to exist, *because* we see it. We have but to lift up our eyes and look around us, and we have proof of it: our eyes tell us.... It is everywhere; and it seems to leave no room for any other world.
>
> And yet in spite of this universal world which we see, there is another world, quite as far-spreading, quite as close to us, and more wonderful; another world all around us, though we see it not, and more wonderful than the world we see, for this reason if for no other, that we do not see it. All around us are numberless objects, coming and going, watching, working or waiting, which we see not: this is that other world, which the eyes reach not unto, but faith only.[229]

In another sermon for Advent he urges the need to be vigilant in an obedience of faith in accordance with Christ's invitation to seek his presence, which is as it were veiled under everything:

> You have to seek His face; obedience is the only way of seeking Him. All your duties are obediences.... Every act of obedience is an approach – an approach to Him who is not far off, though He seems so, but close behind this visible screen of things which hides Him from us. He is behind this material framework; earth and sky are but a veil going between Him and us; the day will come when He will rend that veil, and show Himself to us. And then, according as we have waited for Him, will He recompense us.[230]

The notion of "The Two Worlds" recurs in a poem written in 1862. In contrast to the beauty of God's glory, which faith taught him to long for, Newman saw that "This gaudy world grows pale."[231] In writing this poem he may well have had in mind what John Keble wrote in a hymn containing the words: "Two worlds are ours."[232] Newman looked on everything in the world with "its power to charm" as "a sort of fairy ground" – that is, a playground of rich and abundant illusion and delusions that we delight to distract ourselves in like children. However, in recognizing the need to renounce all this world's delights – whether "The tender memories of the past" or "The hopes of coming years" – he concludes that

> Poor is our sacrifice...
> We offer what we cannot keep,
> What we have ceased to love.[233]

In commenting on Newman's longest poem, *The Dream of Gerontius*, the great Oratorian theologian Louis Bouyer succinctly describes Newman's whole approach and perspective regarding the things of this world:

> Not only does it present us with a most impressive vision of Christian death as introducing us to eternal life, but it is shot through with that sense of the invisible throbbing within the visible world which is so "Newmanian." [...] The fact remains that there is no poem of Newman's where some reminiscence may not be found of his vision of faith – the presence of the invisible behind the visible so characteristic of Newman's religiosity.[234]

From his early days of pastoral ministry as an Anglican to his last as a Roman Catholic, Newman combated every form of tepidity that shies away from seeking to deepen faith – whether this be in not showing enough care in seeking the Truth, indifferentism, or an exaggeration of one's own efforts, capacities and merits. He likewise reproved an evasion of responsibility on the part of people who easily make excuses for their moral weakness, infidelity or laxity.[235] He clearly perceived that whatever be the reason for a person's wallowing in a lukewarm condition, there can be detected not infrequently a certain degree of self-justification, the self-exonerating sin of presumption which, like despair, is against Christian hope.[236] In a sermon preached one Quinquagesima Sunday he challenged his parishioners to shun two snares that deter realizing holiness: laziness and fear:

> we sit coldly and sluggishly at home; we fold our hands and cry "a little more slumber;" we shut our eyes, we cannot see things afar off, we cannot "see the land which is very far off;" we do not understand that Christ calls us after Him; we do not hear the voice of His heralds in the wilderness; we have not the heart to go forth to Him who multiplies the loaves, and feeds us by every word of His mouth.... We fear to be too holy.... The Church is rising up around us day by day towards heaven, and we do nothing but object, or explain away, or criticize, or make excuses, or wonder. We fear to cast in our lot with the Saints, lest we become a party; we fear to seek the strait gate, lest we be of the few not the many.[237]

Far from encouraging an attitude of self-reliance or that of presumption on God's goodness, Newman, as Augustine did centuries earlier, taught that nothing less than a grateful disposition to respond to and cooperate with God's grace calling them to holiness will ensure bringing about the fruition of the deepest desire and hope implanted in the human heart. Thus, for example, in commenting on the Gospel parable of the two sons (cf. Mt 21:28-30) he minced no words about slackness in commitment or indecisiveness that not infrequently is found among Christians:

"Deeds, not words and wishes," this must be the watch-word of your warfare and the ground of your assurance. But if you have done nothing firm and manly hitherto, if you are as yet the coward slave of Satan, and the poor creature of your lusts and passions, never suppose you will one day rouse yourselves from your indolence.[238]

Not to heed and take up this divine invitation, but trifling with con-victions, amounts to a practical atheism; it is tantamount to relying on self unduly rather than on God's grace.[239] Only by divine grace, as St. Paul insisted, we are called, justified, and glorified insofar as becoming conformed to the image of Christ, who revealed God's love from which nothing can separate us (cf. Rm 8:29f.).[240] Rooted in this faith-based truth Newman candidly proclaimed the nature and motive of hope in the first sermon he preached as an ordained Roman Catholic priest after returning to England:

To hope is not only to believe in God, but to believe and be certain that He loves us and means well to us; and therefore it is a great Christian grace. For faith without hope is not certain to bring us to Christ.... "Behold now is the acceptable time; behold now is the day of salvation." This is the day of hope; this is the day of work; this is the day of activity. "The night cometh when no man can work," but we are children of the light and of the day, and therefore despondency, coldness of heart, fear, sluggish-ness are sins in us. Temptations indeed come on you to murmur, but resist them, drive them aside, pray God to help you with His mighty grace. He allows no temptation to befall us which He does not give us grace to surmount. Do not let your hope give way, but "lift up the languid hands and [strengthen] the relaxed knees" (Heb 12:12). "Lose not your confidence, which hath a great reward" (Heb 10:35). Seek His face who ever dwells in real and bodily presence in His Church.[241]

Newman was well-qualified to offer this advice about not losing hope in God's saving action, since he himself had come to a moral certainty that the Church is where it is manifoldly manifest. As he had learned, this certainty, however, is discovered by dint of searching, in which a person is ever divinely prompted and constantly aided. Before becoming a Roman Catholic he had arduously been seeking for certainty about the authentic way in which God's grace is manifest and guaranteed. As a leading member of the Oxford Movement he had thought that this way of sacramental mediation of divine grace lay in the Anglican Church's claim to be "the *Via Media*." But his convictions about this were shattered when his attention was drawn to an article by Nicolas Wiseman, who quoted Augustine's famous sentence that described the situation of schismatics being cut off from the means of truth that unites all in a communion of grace.[242] The following words from the account Newman gave of the impression Augustine's sentence made on him are worth recalling:

> a mere sentence, the words of St. Augustine, struck me with a power which I never had felt from any words before.… [T]hey were like the "Tolle, lege,-Tolle, lege," of the child, which converted St. Augustine himself. "Securus judicat orbis terrarum!" By those great words of the ancient Father… the theory of the *Via Media* was absolutely pulverized.[243]

Recalling a memorandum written on September 7, 1829, he went on to acknowledge that "for years I must have had something of an habitual notion, though it was latent… my mind had not found its ultimate rest, and that in some sense or other I was on journey."[244] He says here that he let himself be led on by God's "kindly light" and "by God's hand blindly, not knowing whither He is taking me," despite "the dismay and disgust which I felt" about a state of doubt and indecisiveness that anguished him. "The one question was" – he says, repeating that existential question that was raised by Paul (cf. Ac

22:10) or the hearers of the apostles' preaching (cf. Ac 2:37; 16:30) – "What was I to do? I had to make up my mind for myself, and others could not help me."[245] In default of having clarity of mind at that stage about whether to leave the Church of England, he determined not to allow himself to be swayed by emotion in following his intuitions and inclinations towards Rome.[246] Alluding to the boy Samuel's being disturbed in the night (cf. 1 S 3:1ff.), he recounts metaphorically that he had sought relief for his anguished state of mind in "sleep again."[247] This avoidance to strive to solve his dilemma about what the Lord was calling him to suggests that he was opting for a line of easiest resistance.

Newman's tarrying to take the step of conversion to the Catholic Church could well be described as a hesitancy to make a leap of faith, to employ Kierkegaard's metaphor. He baulked at all the sacrifices that he foresaw would be required of him. These sacrifices entailed a surrender of many things: the respected teaching position in Oxford, a much valued ministry of preaching at the University church of St. Mary the Virgin, and above all the friendship of many persons he loved and esteemed. In reviewing the dilemma he faced he recalled that he was held back from making this momentous decision by something even stronger than all the losses he foresaw. He says that he was unable to make the further step at any earlier stage until "honestly to say that I was *certain* of the conclusions at which I had already arrived… without doubt and apprehension, that is, with any true conviction of mind or certitude."[248] Greater than honesty or sincerity – for there can be and are many honest fools, whose sincerity is not in question nor can be doubted – what was at issue for him was that of possessing "true conviction of mind or certitude" – a certitude not only about seeking, but in following the truth. This is the gist of his *Apologia* in which he vindicates himself against Canon Charles Kingsley's charge made against him, and generally against Catholic priests. No less than a hundred times in this work mention is made of the word "mind." It is clear that for Newman its proper use, exercise or functioning was a most serious matter. It is interesting to note that whereas in relating his search for certitude about the Catholic Church he speaks about the history of his "opinions," fluctuating and drifting about without assured moorings; however, after telling of his conversion he describes "the position of my mind," that is, the firmness and stability of being rooted in truth.[249] Newman's journey of faith had led him from the evangelical wing to a sacramental approach in the Church of England and eventually to the Catholic Church. The Dominican theologian Aidan Nichols observes:

> As Newman realized in his thoughtful retrospect on the evangelicalism of his youth and early manhood, a religion of the sentiments alone is not only dangerously inadequate when squalls of feeling arise in the storms of life, but also there is the problem that it cannot do justice to the way Christianity has an all-embracing "Idea," the divine revelation with, at its center, the Incarnation of the Word.[250]

Newman could not rest, although he was left without any "positive Anglican theory" and without a theological position.[251] His shift of conscious conviction about becoming a Catholic is not without significance. Describing where he had arrived, he wrote:

> I was not conscious of firmer faith in the fundamental truths of Revelation, or of more self-command; I had not more fervor; but it was like coming into port after a rough sea; and my happiness on that score remains to this day without interruption."[252]

These words recall what years earlier he had said in a sermon, in which the imagery of a turbulent sea journey may well have remained with him from his experience on an orange-boat from Sicily to Marseilles when he wrote "Lead, Kindly Light":

> Here we are tossing upon the sea, and the wind is contrary.
> All through the day we are tried and tempted in various

ways. We cannot think, speak, or act, but infirmity and sin are at hand. But in the unseen world, where Christ has entered, all is peace.... That is our *home*; here we are but on pilgrimage, and Christ is calling us home.[253]

The word "home" had a special resonance for him. Thus, on returning to Birmingham after his investiture as a Cardinal in Rome he said to his community:

To come home again! In that word home how much is included. I know well that there is a more heroic life than a home life. We know how the blessed Apostles went about, and we listen to St. Paul's words – those touching words in which he speaks of himself, and says he was an outcast. Then we know, too, that our blessed Lord had not where to lay his head. Therefore, of course, there is a higher life, a more heroic life than that of home. The idea of home is consecrated to us by our patron and founder, St. Philip, for he made the idea of home the very essence of his religion and institute. There, I do indeed feel pleasure in coming home again.[254]

The home in which he yearned, however, to find ultimately restful peace – that "distant scene" – was always heaven; his conversion to communion with the Catholic Church was the way to realize the fulfillment of his hope for the same peace that Augustine depicts at the end of his *Confessions*. Homesickness may well have been the emotion implicit in his *Home Thoughts Abroad*, written in 1836. In *The Dream of Gerontius* Newman has the Angel tell the soul that the sight of God his Judge will make it "sick with love, and yearn for Him."[255]

Newman's conversion story of becoming a Catholic began in earnest through his thorough perusal of and reflection on the writings of the Fathers, who taught that the Church is born from the Paschal Mystery, sustained through it and brought to fulfillment by it. He found in them that "Catholic truth would bring him safe home, without overstepping the limits of truth and sobriety."[256] The Fathers were, as he put it in verses he had written, "Our fathers and our guides."[257] Newman was at home with these ancient teachers of the truth of God's holy word, which they interpreted authoritatively. He deeply trusted their teaching, for they pointed the direction to the path traced out by the Good Shepherd, about which he said in a sermon:

> Let us not be content with ourselves; let us not make our own hearts our home, or this world our home, or our friends our home; let us look out for a better country, that is a heavenly [one]. Let us look out for Him who alone can guide us to that better country; let us call heaven our home, and this life a pilgrimage; let us view ourselves, as sheep in the trackless desert, who, unless they follow the shepherd, will be sure to lose themselves, sure to fall in with the wolf. We are safe while we keep close to Him, and under His eye.[258]

Here was the home of the hope of certitude for which he longed:

> Our hoping is a proof that hope, as such, is not an extravagance; and our possession of certitude is a proof that it is not a weakness or an absurdity to be certain. How it comes about that we can be certain is not my business to determine; for me it is sufficient that certitude is felt.[259]

I trust and hope most fully

Newman wrote *The Dream of Gerontius* in three weeks. It was published in two parts in the periodical *The Month* in May and June 1865. It became well known through the *Oratorio* composed in 1900 by Sir Edward Elgar, who had been given as a wedding present the copy of it that General Gordon possessed when killed at Khartoum.[260]

By means of a character Gerontius, whose name means "old man,"[261] Newman depicted most clearly his awareness and coming to terms with basic issues that had exercised his mind over the years: that of the relation of human development to time; the question of human immersion in the vicissitudes of time as being accountable before God for eternity; the intriguing interrelation between the visible and invisible worlds.[262] Newman introduces us to a heightened awareness of the transcendent design of God accessible even now, which Henry Vaughan likewise perceived and communicated in his poem "The World":

> I saw Eternity the other night,
> Like a great *Ring* of pure and endless light,
>   All calm, as it was bright.[263]

Newman's lifelong affirmation of hope was about being led kindly by the Lord's light, as he had put it in his famous hymn, towards the communion of divine Love's truth in which we shall see the purity of Light and reflect the Light of Christ coming into the world (cf. Ps 35:10; Jn 1:9). As he put it in recommending the two personalities of the Gospel bearing the name John as patterns of pure sanctity:

> such Saints came so close to the Object of their love, they were granted so to receive Him into their breasts, and so to make themselves one with Him, that their hearts did not so much love heaven as were themselves a heaven, did not so much see light as were light; and they lived among men as those Angels in the old time, who came to the patriarchs and spake as though they were God, for God was in them, and spake by them. Thus these two were almost absorbed in the Godhead, living an angelical life, as far as man could lead one, so calm, so still, so raised above sorrow and fear, disappointment and regret, desire and aversion, as to be the most perfect images that earth has seen of the peace and immutability of God.[264]

In his epic of Gerontius' dream Newman indulges in no idle day-dreaming nor romanticism, but crafts theology into poetry, which quite unlike dry tracts on eschatology or the "Last Things" (death, judgment, heaven, hell) plunges and penetrates into the mystery of personal relationship with God as Dante does in his great masterpiece, to which it has been sometimes more fittingly compared than with Milton's *Paradise Lost*, Tennyson's *In Memoriam*, or other pieces concerning life after death. C.S. Lewis regarded Newman's *Dream* as magnificently presenting the notion of purgatory, for as he put it "the saved soul, at the very foot of the throne, begs to be taken away and cleansed. It cannot bear for a moment longer 'With its darkness to affront that light.'"[265] By means of the biblical literary form of the dream Newman recounts the definitive exodus or Passover from this existence. It has been remarked that it is curious why Newman, who was meticulously careful in his choice of words, especially regarding matters of immense importance, called this work a "dream." Perhaps the reason is simply that out of reverential respect he didn't want his poetic presentation, which dealt with the sacred moment of Gerontius' death (an image of every person's rite of passage), to be taken literally.[266] Decades before Sigmund Freud outlined his theory of dream interpretation and the function of dreams, Newman masterfully shows that a Christian point of view leads to the awakening of genuine hope of eternal salvation, instead of only psychological sanity. *The Dream of Gerontius* is wholly about hope for union with Christ. The grace of Christian hope makes better sense of our anxieties than the inner intuitions of imagination by bringing them into a pattern or harmony, albeit the attempt of poetic imagination in suggesting our problems become resolved in the repose of sleep. Thus, for example, Shakespeare wrote that in nature sleep "knits up the ravell'd sleeve of care."[267] Coleridge for his part exclaimed:

> Oh Sleep! It is a gentle thing,
> Beloved from pole to pole!
> To Mary Queen the praise be given!

> She sent the gentle sleep from Heaven,
> That slid into my soul.[268]

Charles Péguy in a mystical vein alludes to the gracious hope received through sharing Christ's flesh and blood, that hope which was invigorated and raised up after his rest in the tomb:

> But if he sleeps, the bread and wine will become his
> flesh and blood…
> Night, you alone dress wounds.[269]

The tonality of Newman's practical mysticism is evident in this narrative poem, in which he depicts the terrible last ordeal of becoming really contemporary with the Truth of Love – Eternal Love. It presents entry into a state of the further purification of all human desires and deepest hope, that is, being enlightened in a manner that no rational process or development of the mind can attain in human existence. In this state Newman's protagonist Gerontius is enabled to realize a new stage of being, which is announced by the Third Choir of Angelicals, who say: "The chill of death is past, and now / The penance-fire begins."[270] This stage is a reversal, or rather, transformation of what the soul knows at the beginning of the poem: "This chill at heart, this dampness on my brow."[271] This realization recalls St. Paul's defiant challenge: "O death, where is thy victory… thy sting?" (1 Cor 15:55), which John Donne reiterated in his sonnet "Death be not proud, though some have called thee / mighty and dreadful, for thou art not so."[272]

Newman's *Dream* resonates with multiple overtones of the Scriptures, magnificently permeated by the spirit of Christian prayer, in which, though having to stand alone at the gate of heaven, every person looks forward to and expects to be ushered into the great communion of angels, saints, and also friends. Newman thus has Gerontius summon them: "Pray for me, O my friends… O loving friends, your prayers! – 'tis he!"[273] The poem shows him comforted because of the strengthening coming from the intercession of the community of faith, as the sacred author put it: "surrounded by so great a cloud of witnesses… looking to Jesus the pioneer and perfecter of our faith" (Heb 12:1-2). Death as a rite of Passover becomes a be-friending experience as the veil over things of our routine everyday experiences is drawn back so that we behold their true significance, their relationship to God through and in his Word, who makes all things new, as John the Seer of Patmos bore witness (cf. Rv 21:5). Without offering any description of the Triune God before whom he finally comes, Gerontius simply, serenely and adoringly exclaims in surrender: "I go before my Judge. Ah!"[274] Gerontius encounters and addresses the personal Eternal Being, to whom he turns at the beginning of his final most significant stage along his life's journey of conversion, looking on him as the "Lover of souls! Great God!" This is similar, but also quite different, to how St. Francis of Assisi faced his end by charmingly singing the Lord's praise for all his creatures, among whom "our Sister Bodily Death" has a unique place of intimacy in *The Canticle of Brother Sun*. As Owen Cummings wryly says:

> Of course, we do not always get on terribly well with our siblings. Sister Death may be one of the siblings we should like to keep at as far a distance as possible…. The great insight of St. Francis is that death is "neither an enemy to be overcome nor a fate to be accepted, but rather a friend, a kinsman, to be received with all courtesy."[275]

Because of a sense of profound reverence and worship before the awesome Presence of God, Gerontius says that he wishes "To slink away, and hide thee from His sight."[276] This is not servile, but holy fear, properly called "awe." While always imbued with a sense of unworthiness, it also implies the boldness to hope, which is rooted in confidence about God's desire to draw us to himself. In this respect Newman's dramatic poem breathes the spirit of the best of religious sentiment such as expressed by George Herbert. In his famous poem, *Love* (III), the Anglican poet states that though a mere creature of dust and, more, because of being "guilty of dust and sin," the gracious gesture of divine Love welcomes and bids us to approach and partake the banquet prepared from eternity. In *The Dream* there is likewise the same note of deep hope-inspired confidence as Samuel Crossman expressed in a meditation on St. Paul's boast about glorying in nothing except the Cross of Jesus (cf. Gal 6:14).[277]

Newman's life can be regarded as proclaiming the "song of love unknown." His was a song of hope in "the assurance of things hoped for, the conviction of things not seen" (Heb 11:1). He thus clung ardently in faith to the Savior-Lord's truth, which Gerontius at the threshold of departing from the human condition firmly professes: "And I trust and hope most fully / In that Manhood crucified."[278] Because his heart was ever strengthened by the grace, light and life springing forth from the Heart of the Crucified God and "for love of him alone," Newman held in veneration

> Holy Church, as His creation,
> And her teachings, as His own.[279]

Newman pointed out on another occasion that "they who stumble at the Catholic mysteries may be dashed back upon the adamantine rocks which base the throne of the Everlasting, and may wrestle with the stern conclusions of reason, since they refuse the bright consolations of faith."[280] The hope that he encouraged he attributes as effected by the pleading of Mary, the Mother of the Church and Help of Christians. "[I]f the sights of earth intoxicate, and its music is a spell upon the soul," it is she above all, he emphasized, who "offers the Eternal Child for our caress, while sounds of cherubim are heard all round singing from out the fullness of the Divine Glory."[281] He elsewhere outlined the basis of Catholic devotion to Mary in the early Fathers' beliefs about her as "the Second Eve."[282]

Newman's lifelong quest for truth consisted in attempting to assess correctly the complementary functions of reason and faith, science and religion, a humanistic morality and the doctrine of Christ's Gospel of love. This hope alone enables that sense of integration of the respective functions of faith and reason, the spiritual and the intellectual which Newman had discussed in his lectures published in *The Idea of a University*, and which he presented a few years later as the "illative sense" in *An Essay in Aid of a Grammar of Assent*. Through faith-filled hope the skein of fragmentary experiences and impressions, fears, doubts as well as beliefs, convictions, aims, desires and aspirations, is woven together in a person's story of conversion towards fulfillment in the communion of love to which the sacraments of the Catholic Church are oriented. Newman held that there can be no real doubt despite whatever difficulties are experienced by reason in relation to the act of assent in faith. Near the beginning of his work on the development of Christian doctrine, Newman stated: "to be just able to doubt is no warrant for disbelieving."[283] An honest faith is not threatened or shaken by whatever difficulties arising from experience, as Newman famously stated:

> Ten thousand difficulties do not make one doubt, as I understand the subject; difficulty and doubt are incommensurate. There of course may be difficulties in the evidence; but I am speaking of difficulties intrinsic to the doctrines themselves, or to their relations with each other.[284]

Difficulties and doubts – an impetus toward hope

It is not without significance that the words just quoted come in the paragraph immediately before his affirmation of his faith in the doctrine of transubstantiation. He goes on to compare faith in the Real Presence in the Blessed Eucharist with "that majestic Article of the Anglican as well as of the Catholic Creed – the doctrine of the Trinity in Unity."[285] Belief in Christ's presence in the Eucharistic Mystery he regarded as an expression of the constancy as well as a development of the truth of the Incarnation. This mystery entails belief in what the Catholic Church teaches as the guardian of the fullness of divinely revealed truth. Newman severely impugned those who close their eyes and refuse the authority of the Church and trifle with conviction in the pretence of seeking truth.[286]

Newman sought growth in certitude about the gradual unfolding of the essential truth contained implicitly in divine Revelation. In his *Apologia*, after referring to a poem by John Keble about responding in filial freedom, not slavishly, to divine guidance under the "Eye of God's word," he states:

> I did not at all dispute this view of the matter, for I made use of it myself; but was dissatisfied, because it did not go to the root of the difficulty. It was beautiful and religious, but it did not even profess to be logical; and accordingly I tried to complete it by considerations of my own, which are to be found in my University Sermons, Essay on Ecclesiastical Miracles, and Essay on Development of Doctrine.[287]

He then outlines his argument, in which he points out that certainty about recognizing the truth of the Catholic Church is arrived at through exercising a "habit of mind" that seeks to perceive "an *assemblage* of concurring and converging probabilities… according to the constitution of the human mind and the will of its Maker."[288] His very language is convergent and coherent with the vibrant tonality of the Holy Scriptures, as seen in the following sentences which are clearly built around, so to speak, the assembly point of the presence of divine converse:

> as if on set purpose, He [God] has made this path of thought rugged and circuitous above other investigations, that the very discipline inflicted on our minds in finding Him, may mould them into due devotion to Him when He is found. "Verily Thou art a hidden God, the God of Israel, the Savior," is the very law of His dealings with

us. Certainly we need a clue into the labyrinth which is to lead us to Him; and who among us can hope to seize upon the true starting-points of thought for that enterprise, and upon all of them, who is to understand their right direction, to follow them out to their just limits, and duly to estimate, adjust, and combine the various reasonings in which they issue, so as safely to arrive at what it is worth any labor to secure, without a special illumination from Himself? Such are the dealings of Wisdom with the elect soul. "She will bring upon him fear, and dread, and trial; and She will torture him with the tribulation of Her discipline, till She try him by Her laws, and trust his soul. Then She will strengthen him, and make Her way straight to him, and give him joy."[289]

Newman's methodological procedure is comparable to that of Pascal insofar as it is empirical, concrete and also intuitive. It pertained to what he described in terms of the "illative sense."[290] Through this, assent to any particular idea is given by right reason and conviction reached by prudent judgment.[291] Thus, his opus magnum, *An Essay on the Development of Christian Doctrine*, is more than a lengthy dry philosophical argument. It is theology at its best. Through its erudite meandering around theological points or historical facts it has a religious quality in the deepest sense, for it extends an invitation to explore the ways of God's designs and dealings with human beings, whose hearts, Newman demonstrates, can be touched and transformed by his presence overarching and permeating all circumstances and experiences of living, in which he calls them to a dialogue of conversion.

The linchpin of this work is the principle of continuity with the Church's Tradition that stretches back in fidelity to "the very religion which Christ and His Apostles taught."[292] His ideas about the development of this Tradition are traceable to at least 1836.[293] They concerned the far larger issue: the convergence of all inquiries in the phenomenon at the center of history. He said retrospectively in a lecture he gave in 1850 that he had been devoting himself for about a decade to the simple question: Where, what, is that thing in this age which in the first age was the Catholic Church?[294] He came to see and describe the fact that Christian doctrine while germinal in the Scriptures is not wholly or fully restricted to them (as maintained in a narrow "sola scriptura/sola fide" position), but develops through subsequent ages in the Tradition of the Church through worship, the lived and living faith of people ("sensus fidelium"), and theological reflection made explicit in the dogmas of the Magisterium. He summed up the point as follows about doctrinal development, which is not merely a notion or "idea" but a fact:

> It is well known that, though the creed of the Church has been one and the same from the beginning, yet it has been so deeply lodged in her bosom as to be held by individuals more or less implicitly, instead of being delivered from the first in those special statements, or what are called definitions... which are but the expression of portions of the one dogma which has ever been received by the Church, are the work of time; they have grown to their present shape and number in the course of eighteen centuries, under the exigency of successive events, such as heresies and the like, and they may of course receive still further additions as time goes on.[295]

In the opening chapter of his great *Essay* Newman uses the image of a stream to describe the process of the development of ideas in philosophy or belief, but then states this is not entirely appropriate, ending the section with these sentences about this process:

> In time it enters upon strange territory; points of controversy alter their bearing; parties rise and fall around it; dangers and hopes appear in new relations; and old principles reappear under new forms. It changes with

them in order to remain the same. In a higher world it is otherwise, but here below to live is to change, and to be perfect is to have changed often.[296]

It has been suggested that "the closest analogy Newman used was that of a cultural development, the way, that is, of an idea or a complex of ideas, in a society."[297] Cultural development, as Newman would maintain in countering the rationalist spirit taking the field in his day, cannot be seen as devoid of religious aspects or adrift from the flow of the Tradition of the Church. It cannot be studied merely as a history of ideas, while on the other hand caution must be exercised in not reading this history only from a narrow perspective of confessional Christianity. Jaroslav Pelikan puts this well:

> Tradition without history has homogenized all the stages of development into one statically defined truth; history without tradition has produced a historicism that relativized the development of Christian doctrine in such a way as to make the distinction between authentic growth and cancerous aberration seem completely arbitrary.[298]

Newman recognized a tension between doubt and tradition, holding that the latter, however, was never static, but in constant development. This development in Tradition or handing on of faith meant a seeking to understand, as St. Anselm expressed it succinctly.[299] This dynamic movement entails endeavoring in hope to understand the objects believed in by past generations in the course of pursuing and coming to terms with their developmental thrust and process towards belief. In his last Oxford University sermon preached in the church of St. Mary the Virgin on the Feast of the Purification, Thursday, February 2, 1843, Newman pointed to the Virgin Mary as the model and most perfect image of the Church's mission to understand and give form to the divine revealed truth entrusted to it.[300] The text on which he preached was: "But Mary kept all these things and pondered them in her heart" (Lk 2:19).

The Image of the "Wounded Healer"

Newman's lived sense of hope is well-illustrated through his wide and deep perspective of Christian faith in human life's ultimate outcome despite seeming failures during this present existence. Ian Ker cites many examples of this in an article showing Newman's spiritual influence on and encouragement of the poet Gerard Manley Hopkins, whose introspective temperament played a part in tending him to become disheartened when posted to Dublin.[301] Although he was a Jesuit priest, Hopkins was a person struggling to express his perception of God's presence especially in nature, while perhaps also concurring with the whimsical but serious sentiment of Emily Dickinson's sentence: "They say that God is everywhere, and yet we always think of Him as somewhat of a recluse." His poetry shows an almost desperate attempt to communicate with God. On the one hand, he wrote expressing a fascination to "capture" the divine presence, as in his "Eucharistic" poem "The Windhover" or in poems glorifying God for his beauty which, albeit shrouded in mystery, enthralled him in the sacramental dapple of creation. Yet, there are also other poems revealing a soul-turbulent anguish that laments the absence and silence of God to him.[302] Despite trying to translate into verse his conviction of faith and his hope about conversing with God as a friend, nevertheless, he voices the complaint of being perplexed and rebuffed by God's justice, that complaint of anyone whose efforts to act aright are rewarded only by failure and frustration:

> Why do sinner's ways prosper? And why must
> Disappointment all I endeavor end?
> Wert thou my enemy, O thou my friend,
> How wouldst thou worse, I wonder, than thou dost
>   Defeat, thwart me?

His keen relational sensitivity reacted against boxing the divine into dogma and "the dull algebra of schoolmen" regarding approaching the most sublime of mysteries, the Trinity.[303]

In his prioritizing of relationality over rationality Newman was at one with the poet Hopkins. Both Hopkins and Newman shared in common an acute soul-suffering from criticism, neglect of recognition of their talents, sense of failure. Neither of these two men, nevertheless, in any way disputed, disguised or watered down those kernel Christian truths proclaimed in the Gospels and preached vigorously by the Apostle Paul: namely, that the work of human redemption becomes achieved through sharing the Savior's Cross, that the essential necessity consists in losing all to find life, that having part in Jesus' death ensures being united to him in the Resurrection. Newman stated forthrightly: "It is a profound gospel principle that victory comes by yielding. We rise by falling."[304]

This assertion, like many others in a similar vein found in his writing and preaching, bears a similarity to what the poet John Donne expressed in one of his poems:

> And as to others' souls I preached Thy word,
>> Be this my Text, my Sermon to mine owne,
>> Therefore that he may raise the Lord throws down.[305]

Whereas the metaphysical poet was referring to the uplifting saving action of God in our individual lives of physical and spiritual decadence, Newman taught that it is both "the rule of God's Providence that we should succeed by failure" and also part of God's grand design that despite being assailed and cast down by its enemies (whether from outside or even within its ranks) the Church would finally be victorious through following the footsteps of the Crucified Savior Lord. The martyrs and indeed all who embrace the Cross in whatever form it is presented to them in this life of weal and woe have the certain blessed hope that death has been trumped by the event of Christ's rising through dying. In virtue of this event of life-giving love Christians' faith and hope is sustained and is prophetic despite "worldly loss and trouble, however severe and accumulated."[306]

Years before his death Newman's awareness of the process

of ageing is reflected in the following rather wistful sentences he wrote:

> I am an old man; my hair white, my eyes sunk in, and my hand so shriveled that I am sometimes quite startled to see it; – but, when I shut my eyes and merely think, I can't believe I am more than 25 years old, and smile to think how differently strangers must think of me from my own internal feelings.[307]

It is quite normal that a certain degree of sadness, nostalgia, disappointment about physical dwindling of prowess and such like thoughts may at times come to persons in advancing years. To appreciate properly the words just quoted, however, it is necessary to situate them in the context of Newman's life. More than a decade, indeed since turning to Rome, he had no little cause for disappointments that mounted because of various factors: frustrations, criticism and suspicion of what he wrote on the part of Church authorities, the disloyalty of Father Faber and others of the Oratory, loneliness as his few remaining friends departed this life, opposition to his efforts to have the role of the laity recognized and to improve their religious and intellectual level – to say nothing of the general feeling of weariness in continuing conscientiously a task he saw as a God-appointed mission. While acknowledging that God had rewarded him in countless ways, he also noted down statements such as: "he [God] has marked my course with almost unintermittent mortification" or "since I have been a Catholic, I seem to myself to have had nothing but failure, personally."[308] Despite all this, however, he remained steadfast in trusting God and commending himself to the mysterious ways and workings of divine Providence, a recurrent theme in his writings.[309] This is beautifully expressed in a meditation on "Hope in God – Creator":

> God has created me to do Him some definite service; He has committed some work to me which He has not com-

mitted to another. I have my mission – I never may know it in this life, but I shall be told it in the next.… I am a link in a chain, a bond of connection between persons.… He does nothing in vain; He may prolong my life, He may shorten it; He knows what He is about. He may take away my friends, He may throw me among strangers, He may make me feel desolate, make my spirits sink, hide the future from me – still He knows what He is about.[310]

Newman was well accustomed to the Cross. He was appreciated for this by ordinary folk who came to his church in the city of Birmingham, such as a woman who said: "He was very comforting in his instruction on the cross. Poor Father, he knows well how to speak of the cross."[311] In all that he lived through during "The Years of Silence,"[312] when his capabilities were overlooked and his potential contribution not called upon by the Church he loved and to which he humbly submitted himself, Newman deepened his personal acquaintance with the mystery of the crucified and wounded Healer, Jesus Christ. This schooled him to appreciate that hope is not a matter of fleeting and febrile moments of enthusiasm, but rather, of perseverance in waiting, patience in rising above personal hurts and injuries in order to show compassion towards others in a Christ-like way. The lesson he himself had assimilated he passed on to others:

If we shrink from suffering and start aside, we are novices in the school of Christian hope – The prospect of future glory should *fill* the mind – what a poor perception of it have we, if it does not strengthen us to submit ourselves with composure to the ills of this life![313]

It was after years of attempting to describe the relation between reason and faith that he succeeded in completing his *An Essay in Aid of a Grammar of Assent*, a work that was no mere exercise in "paper logic" but one that gives a feeling for higher realities than those graspable by reason. These realities he experienced in the existential drama of human anguish that he understood in relation to the logic of the Crucified Lord's love. Newman's fidelity to this experience thus enabled him to write the following sentences:

> the universal Deliverer, long expected, when He came,… instead of making and securing subjects by a visible graciousness or majesty, departs; – *but* is found, through His preachers, to have imprinted the Image or idea of Himself in the minds of His subjects individually; and that Image, apprehended and worshipped in individual minds, becomes a principle of association, and a real bond of those subjects one with another, who are thus united to the body by being united to that Image.… It is the Image of Him who fulfils the one great need of human nature, the Healer of its wounds, the Physician of the soul, this Image it is which both creates faith, and then rewards it.[314]

These words are in perfect accord with the sentiment expressed by Gogol about the lasting impression made on persons through history by humankind's Savior, who comes "not in proud splendor and majesty, not as the avenger of wickedness, not as a judge come to destroy some and reward others" but "with the gentle kiss of a brother… as only God could come, as the prophets who had been inspired by God had represented Him, divinely."[315] There is no doubt that Newman was certainly right in his view about the "Image" of such a Savior signifying more for the run-of-the-mill human beings than all the royal divine titles and attributes discussed by theologians and enshrined in the dogmas of the Church. Newman would have concurred entirely with Pope Paul VI's perspicacious observation that may have been in a certain sense even applicable in his day as it is in our own, namely, that people sated by talk have passed beyond the "civilization of the word" and live "in the civilization of the image."[316] Newman was sensitively aware that people are drawn by the pathos and beauty of God's nearness revealed, that is, unveiled in this icon of his compassion. It is this above all that shows the credibility of divine love in the midst of human suffering; it is this that ultimately provokes unanswerable questions twisted around the problem of pain. A poet who lived through the tortured times of war and searing hopelessness, T.S. Eliot, attempted to give what is no answer to the question of pain, but merely a pointer to the heart of its mystery:

> Who then devised the torment? Love.
> Love is the unfamiliar Name
> Behind the hands that wove
> The intolerable shirt of flame
> Which human power cannot remove.[317]

Newman presented this divine mystery of love as the sole sustaining support of hope that enables humankind to rise to join the angelic choirs in praising God, who is "Most sure in all his ways":

> O wisest love! that flesh and blood / Which did in Adam fail,
> Should strive afresh against the foe, / Should strive and
>   should prevail;
> And that a higher gift than grace / Should flesh and blood
>   refine,
> God's presence and His very Self, / And Essence all-divine.[318]

As a pastor he was adroit in his apposite use of imagery and analogies from nature, the force of which is readily appealing insofar as he indicated the continuity between God's creative action in nature and his condescension in offering Christ's healing grace. He saw clearly this continuity as intrinsically part of divine Providence's overseeing magnificent redemptive design and finest achievement.[319] All things, all aspects of living – especially the most irksome and painful – are under the overarching grace of God, the presence of which when recognized in faith leads to a greater response in love and to a trusting hope that because of the divine graciousness all will be well in the end. Faith deepened by encountering the incarnate Crucified Savior flows lovingly into the realization of hope concerning the as yet unseen, but assured by the mysterious divine dispensation (or *Economia* as the Greek Fathers of the Church called it).[320] Newman explains:

> As Almighty God did not all at once introduce the Gospel to the world, and thereby gradually prepared men for its profitable reception, so, according to the doctrine of the early Church, it was a duty, for the sake of the heathen among whom they lived, to observe a great reserve and caution in communicating to them the knowledge of "the whole counsel of God." This cautious dispensation of the truth, after the manner of a discreet and vigilant steward, is denoted by the word "economy." It is a mode of acting which comes under the head of Prudence, one of the four Cardinal Virtues.[321]

These sentences succinctly express how the Church's pastoral practice from early times – the so-called discipline of secrecy about the sacred truths of the Creed and sacraments or mysteries (*disciplina arcani*)[322] – is in conformity and continuity with God's own action of gradually disclosing his design to enlighten and prepare humankind to receive the Gospel. This gradual process of the divine dispensation, Newman points out, moreover, "had a definite application to the duties of Christians, whether clergy or laity, in preaching, in instructing or catechizing, or in ordinary intercourse with the world around them."[323] It is appropriate to indicate here that the idea expressed in these words became an important theme in the Second Vatican Council's understanding of and outreach to non-Christian religious beliefs, in which there are already seeds of the Gospel (*praeparatio evangelii*).[324] This idea implies the need for sensitivity in responsible missionary activity, which should not be merely proselytizing.

Newman's teaching concerning a diligent and prudent preaching of the Gospel spelled out a message of hope insofar as it pointed to the need of human beings to be brought into that at-onement of all creation becoming related through coming under the headship of Christ, as St. Paul described (cf. Rm 8:18ff.; Eph 1:9f.).[325] His sermons were aimed at convincing the hesitant, confirming and strengthening the weak and weary, comforting those in need of solace and pastoral solicitude. Love, he understood from personal experience, is that "wound in the soul" that could only be healed by the divine touch.[326] Newman insisted on the importance in preaching about turning the people's gaze to look to Christ, who by entering our sorry state of separation from God relates human beings to the wellspring of God's grace. He was thus opposed to what had become a fashionable style of preaching in certain circles, where he deplored a focusing on and whipping up of feelings about being converted as an end in itself, which obstructs and obfuscates contemplating Christ, since he – rather than our ephemeral and subjective sentiments about him or, worse, about some intense feeling of being saved – is humankind's unique hope of glory. In *The Dream of Gerontius*, the Angel tells the soul:

> It is the face of the Incarnate God
> Shall smite thee with that keen and subtle pain;
> And yet the memory, which it leaves, will be
> A sovereign febrifuge to heal the wound;
> And yet withal it will the wound provoke,
> And aggravate and widen it the more.[327]

Although the pain of being wounded is only intensified by beholding God's healing face of love, although thrown into confusion and bewilderment, the soul responds that it prefers not "to disengage the tangle" of the angelic words to it by seeking to impose an interpretation of its own on these sublime mysteries. Newman here touches on a truth experienced by the greatest mystics.[328]

Heart speaks unto heart

The pastoral objective in preaching according to Newman really amounts to calling people to hope, not merely by use of logical argumentation or "a smart syllogism," but by touching their hearts.[329] Newman preferred to stay close to concrete experience shared by ordinary people. He drew an important distinction between what he calls "notional" and "real" assent. In this he tended to have little patience with the approach of logicians, saying that

> Logic makes but sorry rhetoric with the multitude.... After all, man is *not* a reasoning animal; he is a seeing, feeling, contemplating, acting animal.... Life is not long enough for a religion of inferences; we shall never have done beginning, if we determine to begin with proof. We shall ever be laying our foundations; we shall turn theology into evidences, and divines into textuaries.... If we insist on proofs for everything, we shall never come to action: to act you must assume, and that assumption is faith.[330]

He understood well that in this manner a preacher could raise the hearts of his hearers to appreciate the final and full scope of human existence, namely, that of entering into an intimate relationship of communion with Jesus Christ in his Mystical Body. It is this communion that God the Father reveals and brings about through and in the Spirit of the Christ, who is the unique Savior of humankind's sinful wounded condition. The word "wound" is obviously used here in two different senses, the first referring to that of divine Love, the other to the state of human beings resulting from not responding to or rejecting God's countless gifts and passionate outreach to them. William Johnston puts this well: "That wounded stag is Jesus himself. He is wounded because we are wounded. He is wounded with love."[331] The notion of the "wounded Healer" is reflected in various places of Newman's writings, in which two of his sermons in particular vividly express it: one preached as an Anglican on "The Incarnate Son, a Sufferer and Sacrifice" and the other preached years later as a Catholic priest on "Mental Sufferings of Our Lord in His Passion."[332]

Among the various replies given to the question about the Church's office or responsibility as a dispenser of God's word, Newman pointed out that the object and purpose of Christian preaching and instructing consists in what St. Paul says about calling and challenging people by that word, in which they are motivated by one reason particularly, that they become God's "elect" (cf. 2 Tm 2:10). The condition for this is that a preacher must work arduously and bear the sufferings of others, for which he should have a deep empathy:

> He [Paul] labored more than all the Apostles; and why? not to civilize the world, not to smooth the face of society, not to facilitate the movements of civil government, not to spread abroad knowledge, not to cultivate the reason, not for any great worldly object, but "for the elect's sake." He "endured all things," all pain, all sorrow, all solitariness; many a tear, many a pang, many a fear, many a disappointment, many a heartache, many a strife, many a wound... he spoke to the many that he might gain the few; he mixed with the world that he might build up the Church; he "endured all things," not for the sake of all men, but "for the elect's sake," that he might be the means of bringing them to glory.[333]

For Newman the standard set is high, indeed the highest both as regards what is hoped for as well as the kind and quality of the content of what should be preached. In this he was not being pessimistic, but realistic. Albeit the aim of Christian preaching consists in desiring and working for the conversion of the whole world, this aim, he held, would be jettisoned if it meant a lowering of the highest values of the Gospel and compromising these with an ethic of mere external conformism, or sense of duty and being useful to society in the eyes of this world, such as prevailed in his day and passed for Christianity. As he put it:

how mistaken is the notion of the day, that the main undertaking of a Christian Church is to make men good members of society, honest, upright, industrious, and well-conducted; and that it fails of its duty, and has cause of shame unless it succeeds in doing so.... The Gospel then has come to us, not merely to make us good subjects, good citizens, good members of society, but to make us members of the New Jerusalem, and "fellow-citizens with the saints and of the household of God." Certainly no one is a true Christian who is not a good subject and member of society; but neither is he a true Christian if he is nothing more than this. If he is not aiming at something beyond the power of the natural man, he is not really a Christian, or one of the elect.[334]

Throughout all his writing, but especially in his sermons, Newman lucidly expressed his perception about the priority of religious relatedness in love as the wellspring of authentic morality. In his outline of a theology of preaching he quotes the advice of St. Francis de Sales that goes back to St. Paul's approach about the spiritual good of people being best served by emphasizing the vitalizing primacy of love in their Christian *being* as the basis of behavior.[335] In a sermon he delivered in Birmingham, he stated that any other motive – vainglory, ambition to exercise authority or power and so on – would be unworthy of a preacher, whose sole task should consist in converting people to Christ and to his Church, in which they, the preachers themselves, should seek to deepen their intimate friendship with humankind's Savior. A preacher should therefore readily communicate the joy he has derived from the treasures of the Gospel:

"Freely ye have received, freely give;" because we dare not hide in a napkin those mercies, and that grace of God, which have been given us, not for our own sake only, but for the benefit of others.[336]

In another sermon he recalled that salvation is found in the Catholic Church since in it there is "a universal remedy" for the disease of sinfulness.[337] Near the end of this sermon he was not mealy-mouthed, but forthrightly threw out a challenge to the congregation about heeding and responding to what is preached:

> the truth must be spoken – we do not need you, but you need us; it is not we who shall be baffled if we cannot gain you, but you who will come short, if you be not gained. Remain, then, in the barrenness of your affections, and the decay of your zeal, and the perplexity of your reason, if you will not be converted.[338]

He pointed out that the preacher's art does not consist in excelling in eloquence or rhetorical skill, making a display of human accomplishment or learning with "the persuasive words of human wisdom," for quoting St. Paul – whom he highly esteemed as most "successful… natural… unstudied… self-forgetting" – "the kingdom of God is not in speech, but in power [1 Cor 4:20]."[339] For this reason he went on to recommend "the very presence of simple earnestness" that is "in itself a powerful natural instrument to effect that toward which it is directed." His choice of the word "earnestness" needs comment. By it he doesn't mean a show of his own intensity of subjective feelings that a preacher imposes on his congregation. As mentioned above, he held as abhorrent any form of exaggerated emotionalism that in revivalist preaching tended to be lightweight on doctrinal orthodoxy.[340] This didn't mean that he was averse to zeal, on the one hand, or that he recommended tepidity or insipid boring preaching, on the other. But, the significance of his use of "earnestness," would seem to suggest rather "seriousness," "reality," or even "pledge," "guarantee," "voucher." This sense of "earnestness" is borne out by what he put in a balanced way in an early sermon:

> Some persons answer at once and without hesitation, that "to have faith is to feel oneself to be nothing, and God

everything; it is to be convinced of sin, to be conscious one cannot save oneself, and to wish to be saved by Christ our Lord; and that it is, moreover, to have the love of Him warm in one's heart, and to rejoice in Him, to desire His glory, and to resolve to live to Him and not to the world." But I will answer, with all due seriousness, as speaking on a serious subject, that this is *not* faith…. Why? Because there is an immeasurable distance between feeling right and doing right. A man may have all these good thoughts and emotions, yet (if he has not yet hazarded them to the experiment of practice) he cannot promise himself that he has any sound and permanent principle at all. If he has not yet acted upon them, we have no voucher, barely on *account* of them, to believe that they are anything but words.[341]

In describing the qualities of a preacher Newman here emphasized the importance of being transparent and coherent in his life with what is uttered. This draws people more readily than any eloquence. He himself bore witness to God's providential faithfulness as a dispenser of divine grace, overseer of his people's needs and also an intercessor in lifting them up in prayer before God's loving merciful kindness.[342] He thus inspired confidence and won the trust of his hearers by living out the well-worn expression: practicing what he preached. While appreciating that even the best of people can waver and falter,[343] he maintained the importance of being steady of purpose and stable in manner of living: "I have ever made consistency the mark of a Saint."[344] The task behooving a preacher, as he clearly saw, thus involves patience and perseverance in confronting both in his flock as well as in himself a residual sluggishness and feebleness of will to obey God because of inveterate, ingrained sinful habitual ways of acting and modes of being:

the Minister of Christ has to teach His sinful people a perfect obedience; and does not know how to set about it, or how to insist on any precept, so as to secure it from being misunderstood and misapplied. He sees men are acting upon low motives and views, and finds it impossible to raise their minds all at once, however clear his statements of the Truth. He feels that their good deeds might be done in a much better manner.... So is it with all of us, Ministers as well as people; it is so with the most advanced of Christians while in the body, and God sees it.[345]

Apart from warning against lethargy in spiritual seriousness, Newman's "chief target" in his preaching was "spiritual complacency," for, "outward behavior, however good, for example, is no guarantee of anything."[346] He impugned self-righteousness of any kind, particularly that detestable form of the falsity of middle-class Victorian "respectability" which was considered the mark of being religious. This arrogance in attitude – in which sins are hidden and disguised, conscience is stifled – deprived persons of a due awe in humility before God, to whom alone the honor of worship and adoration is due. Being vigilant and prayerful in hope is a frequent theme in his preaching.[347] Many years later at the university church in Dublin he said:

> one of these characteristics of a Christian spirit, springing from the three theological virtues, and then in turn defending and strengthening them, is that habit of waiting and watching ... and the same habit is also a mark of the children of the Church, and a note of her divine origin.[348]

In advocating a thorough-going Christocentric spirituality Newman deplored every form of self-contemplation or introspectiveness, that method of self-analysis inculcated by the Evangelicals, from whom nevertheless, as the scholar Ian Ker points out,[349] he had learned the importance of giving due place to a discernment and purification of motives. Only in this way an adequate response could be freely made to Christ, who as God's unique Word of hope enlightens and clarifies the human heart's divinely implanted desire for wellbeing. It was, thus, not merely a matter of being true to oneself, as in Polonius' last word of advice to his son Laertes.[350] Rather, like Augustine's search for interiority,[351] Newman advocated discernment or scrutiny of the heartland of self insofar as this sharpened one's focus on the hope of discovering and entering into a deeper, more loving relationship with the divine presence: "As men in a battle cannot see how it is going, so Christians have no certain signs of God's presence in their hearts, and can but look up towards their Lord and Savior, and timidly hope.[352]

To awaken and stir up a desire in others for their spiritual good was the burden of Newman's constant concern. This meant leading people to know themselves before God, to recognize and be grateful for being led towards realizing their true calling to holiness, wherein they experience personally the Lord's transforming paschal dynamism drawing and impelling them into the mystery of God's loving design for all humankind.[353] He discharged his ministry with pastoral responsibility urged on by charity (cf. 2 Cor 5:14). He envisaged the purpose of education in fostering knowledge "worth possessing for what it is, and not merely for what it does" – valued for leading to a sense of the beauty of truth.[354] As Louis Bouyer put it:

> We may observe… the same preoccupations, the same sense of responsibility in educational matters.… He was the one to whom the younger folk looked for guidance, to help them in this life, and to show them the path to the next; to find themselves, and to find God.[355]

Keenly interested in a humanistic educative process, Newman translated the thrust of this process into religious Christian terms as a conscientious movement of conversion, which he saw related to three other themes that constantly occupied his focus of attention: revelation, the Church, and dogma.[356] He was also sensitive in appreciating realities glimpsed from childhood beneath the surface of appearances. Recalling his own early experience, he stated beautifully in one of his sermons:

> this we know full well – we know it from our own rec-
> ollection of ourselves, and our experience of children
> – that there is in the infant soul, in the first years of its
> regenerate state, a discernment of the unseen world in the
> things that are seen, a realization of what is Sovereign
> and Adorable.[357]

His wistful dreams of childhood may have been wishful think-ing,[358] but they eventually took him towards genuine hoping through his docility to the Spirit of Christ who shaped his complex person-ality into the simplicity of freedom experienced only by those who delight in and marvel like children at the invisible wonders wrought by God our Father.

Particularly from the days when he was a leading light in the Tractarian Oxford Movement, his focus was directed to the sacra-mental economy of redemptive grace mediated through the Church's liturgy, which is a solid and reliable *locus theologicus*. The ancient adage *Lex orandi lex credendi* was foundational in his approach to the proclamation of the mystery of God's word in order to lead to an ever deeper abundant life of faith, which when lived in love opens the way to experience even here and now a glimpse of the hoped-for eternal reality of God's kingdom. This approach to preaching in Newman is in perfect accord with what Pope Benedict XVI speaks of regarding the purpose of the homily in the liturgy as fostering a deep and per-sonal sense of relationship with Christ – a sense of "contemporaneity" much emphasized by Pope John Paul II.[359] This sense was Newman's constant and unswerving focus, the truth of mystery that is actually unfolded and resounding through the Church's proclamation and cel-ebration of God's holy word. In this regard Professor Nicholas Lash's words are relevant: "The *fides quaerens intellectum* thus continually seeks to unify all our experience and understanding, 'secular' as well as 'religious,' in the light of that one mystery."[360]

Newman's exercise of the art of preaching throughout his ministry may be regarded as a pastoral attempt of faith seeking to understand and integrate all human experience into the divine revelation, that overarching economy of hope. Many who had heard him preach at the university church of St. Mary the Virgin observed that his sermons, apart from their beauty as prose and mastery in use of English, offer a clarity and depth of teaching on Christian spirituality, which, though present, is not readily evident in his more theological writing. He didn't go in for the devices employed in pulpit oratory of the day, except for a long pause occasionally in order to arrest the attention of his listeners and to give them an opportunity to reflect upon and assimilate a point he was making.[361] He used simple words that were uttered with a deliberate and musical quality of his voice that gently pierced the silence and made an unforgettable impression on those who heard him.[362] His sermons as a Catholic priest at the Birmingham Oratory, different from his Oxford preaching, were not read; the record of these exist only in notes as an *aide memoire* that he used.[363] In preaching and teaching the faith Newman always addressed the hearts of people, which he sought to touch and transform and raise up in hope to be in communion with one another in the worship of God, who communicates through a minister's faithful service of his holy Word and Spirit: "heart speaks unto heart."

Paschal dynamism of hope

The whole movement of John Henry Newman's long life can be seen summed up in two phrases: *"Heart speaks unto heart"* and *"From shadows and appearances into Truth."*[364] Together they may be taken as expressing his ever-resilient Christian hope. The first was the motto he chose for his coat of arms when created a cardinal by Pope Leo XIII in 1879.[365] It epitomizes well the warmth and sincere personal tone of his gift to communicate to others what he had constantly sought attentively from the depths of God's love – that hope-inspiring love which he found especially in the Eucharistic Presence, the Mystery of Faith. This is expressed in a prayer he wrote:

> O most Sacred, most loving Heart of Jesus, Thou art concealed in the Holy Eucharist, and Thou beatest for us still. Now as then Thou sayest, *Desidero desideravi* – With desire I have desired.... O make my heart beat with Thy Heart. Purify it of all that is earthly, all that is proud and sensual, all that is hard and cruel, of all perversity, of all disorder, of all deadness. So fill it with Thee, that neither the events of the day nor the circumstances of the time may have power to ruffle it, but that in Thy love and Thy fear it may have peace.[366]

The words *"From shadows and appearances into Truth"* that Newman directed to be inscribed on his tombstone express not merely a wish for deliverance from the unreality of all this world's deceptions.[367] Rather, they imply a perception that there exists the Reality of God, whose love does not and will never cheat us of the desire for Truth, that inalienable right he has etched into us as a heartfelt longing in hope. While the source of this phrase is difficult to trace, its perspective is clearly that of the (neo) Platonist approach of many of the Fathers of the Church which influenced Newman's manner of looking on the sense objects of human perception.[368] He regarded everything of this world not in a negative way, however, but as imbued with a potential for conveying ultimate truths and leading to sharing in the mysteries of God. The entire focus of theology in Newman's understanding is oriented towards and colored by God's design, the supreme purpose of which is revealed in and through the mystery of the Incarnate Christ, "the image of the invisible God, the first-born of all creation" (Col 1:15). He cites this text, together with various other pertinent verses from the Fourth Gospel, in order to highlight the quality of Christ in being the unique Way to understand that the end of human existence is not in the passing things of this world, but to behold and participate in the glory of communion with the Holy Trinity.[369]

In other words, the dynamic thrust of human living – a conversion curve toward Christ – is ever onwards, pointing and pressing us towards giving priority to the responsibility of seeking the kingdom of God; and theology, which Newman valued as among the highest and noblest of human endeavors and activities,[370] consists in pondering on and contemplating all experience of created being in relation to God's wonderful purpose, which calls us to participate in the divine being-in-communion. This is the fullness of truth into which, as Newman repeatedly taught, we are being led by the Holy Spirit, whom the Father graciously sends in response to the prayer that Jesus uttered while entering into the climactic moment of his Paschal Mystery (cf. Jn 14:16, 26; 15:26; 16:7ff.). The glorious truth of our being-in-communion with Christ and with one another, this is what we are enabled to discern and acknowledge as we *passover* through the shadows and oftentimes deceptive appearances of our present experiences.

At various places in Newman's writings or sermons, echoes can be heard of the phrase *"From shadows and appearances into Truth."* Thus, for instance, Newman has the Angel tell the soul in *The Dream of Gerontius*:

> Nor touch, nor taste, nor hearing hast thou now;
> Thou livest in a world of signs and types,
> The presentations of most holy truths,
> Living and strong, which now encompass thee.[371]

Ronald Knox cites the words of Newman's epitaph in one of his sermons preached for the feast of Corpus Christi.[372] In a similar way to Newman, he goes on to comment that in the Sacrament of the Eucharist we behold as through a chink "the light of the other world." This catches well a recurrent theme expressed by Newman, who understood and presented the sacramentality of the Eucharistic Mystery as offering the clue, and more than a mere clue, already a shadow, copy, and indeed foretaste of the abundant reality of eternal life, which Jesus promised and communicated in the Gospels.

Newman's life – as symbolically caught in the phrase *"Ex umbris et imaginibus in veritatem"* like that other one, *"Cor ad cor loquitur"* – can thus be recognized as expressing the paschal dynamism of hope. His life was a journey focused on seeking to witness to the reality communicated in the greatest and most central Christian celebration of the Easter Sacrament. For here, we pass from the dark shadows of this world's night, and, as in the ritual and imagery of the Church's liturgy of the great Easter Vigil, we proclaim our gratitude and praise God for his involvement in and transformation of human history through Christ, the true Light of the world, whose Spirit unites us in communion with him and our brothers and sisters.

Ecumenical vision of ecclesial hope

At the beginning of this chapter Pope Paul VI's words of high tribute were cited regarding Newman's perspicacity in dealing with many problems requiring sensitive attention. Although not always understood and sometimes misinterpreted in his own time, Newman anticipated issues approached by the Second Vatican Council: religious liberty and inviolability of conscience, which as he argued was a precious indicator enabling "real" – not merely "notional" – assent to the existence of God in a personal way of commitment better than that shown by the traditional "proofs" of scholastic philosophical theology;[373] the role of the laity;[374] the importance of Christian education; the relationship between the Church and the world; the crucial responsibility to pray and work to bring about unity among people through dialogue with fellow Christians, members of world religions, as well as with all persons of good will.[375]

Newman had no ecumenical project as such. Yet, the focus of his thought was ever related to the vital questions of the Christian Church's unity and its mission to foster holiness. As he put it in a hymn he firmly held in veneration for the love of Christ, "Holy

Church, as his creation, / And her teachings, as his own." His confidence in having made the right decision in becoming a Catholic impelled him to seek to bring others to what he considered to be the true Church. His first fervor as a convert made him repudiate the Anglican variety of positions as a consequence of lacking the firmness of authority he found in the Roman Church.[376] Nevertheless, as the years passed he mellowed and expressed his appreciation for many of the rich features of the tradition in the Church of England, an inheritance about which, as Professor Owen Chadwick says, never before had any Roman Catholic written with greater generosity than Newman did in responding to Canon Charles Kingsley's charge about Catholic priests not caring for truth. However, Chadwick remarks, his ecumenical outlook was weak and, while cordial to those seeking reunion of the Church of England and Rome, he did not join in their endeavors; he saw neither how this reunion could happen nor an answer to the vexed question of the validity of Anglican orders.[377]

During his visit to Britain Pope Benedict XVI paid tribute to Newman's ecclesial vision that his Anglican background and years of ministry in the Church of England had nurtured and brought to maturity. He added that lessons can be learned from Newman about virtues required by ecumenism: the following of conscience without counting the cost; maintaining a warmth of continued friendship with former colleagues in exploring with them "in a truly eirenical spirit, the questions on which they differed, driven by a deep longing for unity in faith."[378] This yearning for unity entails seeking "the faith of the Church"[379] through conscientious and prayerful commitment together with others in a quest, such as Newman exemplified, to discover the implications of the depths of the truth of communion with God revealed by Christ. In this responsible task of dialogue that entails openness to what the Word reveals and God's Holy Spirit is saying to the churches (cf. Rv 3:6), Christians have as their model the Blessed Virgin Mary, for, as Newman said:

> she symbolizes to us, not only the faith of the unlearned,
> but of the doctors of the Church also, who have to inve-

stigate, and weigh, and define, as well as to profess the Gospel.[380]

In following the example of Mary, the Mother of the Church and Help of Christians, the fruits of ecumenism will come to light in the gracious growth of a sense of "brotherhood rediscovered."[381] Newman sought to realize this brotherhood through fostering the marriage of faith and reason, an interfacing of the complementary components and contributions of religion and secular knowledge. He understood profoundly that for this "marriage" to succeed a dialogue that was open and ongoing had to be entered into and maintained with great care. True dialogue meant for him seeing another person's point of view.[382] This is most pertinent when intellectually divergent approaches exist not only between Christians, but also between believers and persons who are unbelievers or agnostic and whose attitude or "habit of mind" is of a rationalistic bent. There would be a dawning of hope for reconciliation when dialogue properly speaking is sought between such persons. This dialogue would be "ecumenical" in the radical and most wide-ranging sense of this word, which means universal or catholic in scope. With a breadth of vision that countermanded every form of stifling anti-intellectualism (the death knell of faith and hope) Newman placed the whole enterprise of setting up a Catholic University in Dublin under the patronage of Blessed Mary ever Virgin, the "Seat of Wisdom" (*Sedes Sapientiae*), in whose honor he built on St. Stephen's Green a beautiful church dedicated under this title. In the first sermon he preached from the pulpit of this church, which was on the feast of Augustine's mother, Monica, he pointed out how appropriate it was that it was the day on which the academic year began, for a university has a role like a mother, for which it is called "Alma Mater." In this role he said that a university's model should be "that greatest and most heavenly of mothers… on the one hand, 'Mater Amabilis,' and 'Causa nostrae laetitiae,' and on the other, 'Sedes Sapientiae' also."[383] He described university education as fostering not only the cultivation of the mind through the various literary and scientific disciplines, but also, through introduction to the "science of sciences" – namely, religious knowledge – the development of the moral and spiritual dimensions and welfare of persons.[384]

Just as the Holy Spirit inspires and guides all learning, so too, as the renowned Newman scholar Ian Ker states, it is very significant that the working of the Spirit of God has become increasingly evident in the emergence of the new Ecclesial Movements since the Second Vatican Council. If these movements "make the central meaning of *Lumen Gentium* clearer and stronger," Ker adds, "they also represent another kind of development in Newman's terms, a reaction against both a clericalized and a laicized Church."[385] This statement, at first seemingly provocative, must be understood as pointing to the overarching unifying principle of baptism, from which spring all the charisms, vocations and ministries of Christ's faithful, who comprise, as Newman taught, both lay and clerical members of the communion of Christ's Mystical Body.[386] The fundamental grace of baptism in Christ holds a primacy over canonical status, as necessary as this is for the institutional visibility and functioning of the Church. Insofar as the baptismal grace orients towards a growth and deepening of the Eucharistic community, however, it can be recognized as enabling the extension of the mystical reality of communion between God and humankind that was revealed by the Incarnation, which for Newman was "the central aspect of Christianity" and "the central truth of the Gospel."[387] The Ecclesial Movements, having the blessing of recent popes, foster the realization of the Second Vatican Council's great ecclesiological insight and teaching on the mystery of the Church as a dynamic icon of the communion of Persons in the divine Trinity as a life-giving and lived experience.[388] This Spirit-guided experiential reality revealed by Christ is the communion toward which all Christians are called. It is the goal of the transcendent hope in humankind's yearning for the truth and beauty of spirituality and holiness that was the focus in the teaching and whole life of Blessed John Henry Newman.

Postlude

Hearts Aflame with Hope
Pope John Paul II and Mother Teresa

Hope is not empty optimism springing from a naive confidence that the future will necessarily be better than the past. Hope and trust are the premise of responsible activity and are nurtured in that inner sanctuary of conscience where "man is alone with God" and he thus perceives that he is not alone amid the enigmas of existence, for he is surrounded by the love of the Creator!

Pope John Paul II[389]

Karol Wojtyla has looked into the heart of virtually every modern darkness and has come out on the far side of that encounter as a "witness to hope," as he described himself at the United Nations in 1995.

Hope is not optimism, which is a matter of optics, of how you look at things. Hope is a sturdier reality, a theological virtue. John Paul II's hope in the human capacity, under grace, to fulfill modernity's great aspiration to freedom and his hope that the future can bring a springtime of the human spirit have been powerful forces in the last two decades of this century of tears.   *George Weigel*[390]

In order to help us deserve heaven, Christ set a condition: At the moment of our death, you and I, whoever we might have been and wherever we have lived, Christians and non-Christians alike, every human being who has been created by the loving hand of God in His own image, shall stand in His presence and be judged according to what we have been for the poor, what we have done for them. Here a beautiful standard for judgment presents itself. We have to

become increasingly aware that the poor are the hope of humanity,
for we will be judged by how we have treated the poor.

Mother Teresa of Calcutta[391]

The saints were able to make the great journey of human existence
in the way that Christ had done before them, because they were
brimming with great hope. *Pope Benedict XVI*[392]

Two of the keynote speakers at the 41st International Eucharistic
Congress at Philadelphia in August 1976, during the Bicentennial
celebrations of the United States of America, were Mother Teresa
of Calcutta and Karol Cardinal Wojtyła from Krakow. The central
theme of this event was "The Eucharist and the Hungers of the Human
Family." Their lives, though very diverse, were united as outstanding
witnesses to the significance of the name of that city: "brotherly love"
that Jesus had commanded as the hallmark of his followers at the Last
Supper. They eloquently spoke of those most basic hungers – material
and spiritual – as intrinsically related to the Eucharist. They pointed
to God's Bread that Christ gave for the life of the world, a unique
Gift which both awakens and also assuages, as no other food can, the
hunger for hope divinely-etched deeply in the human heart.

When he became pope a few years later as John Paul II, Karol
Wojtyła taught all people to recognize and respect one another's
dignity by working together for justice and peace, sustained by the
substantial bread of true life that comes down from heaven (cf. Jn
6:41, 58). Like that "man from a far country,"[393] the humble nun of
Albanian origin provided the bread of hope to people of all ages and
every condition of life: married couples, those in the priestly ministry
and religious life, persons searching for meaning in life, those outside
the Christian faith, whether Jews or Moslems, Buddhists or atheists,
and especially countless young persons, whose hearts they both inspired and set aflame with a sense of mission about their calling to
be the future and the hope of the Church. This Polish pope and this
woman showed that the attitude in which life's work is undertaken

shapes human beings into who they are according to God's design of love. Their tireless endeavors demonstrated that secular activities become truly sacred through being offered at the Eucharistic Sacrifice in unity with Christ's own supremely loving gift of himself. They were thus both truly ecumenical, Eucharistic-hearted persons.

Hope – the divine work of mercy

In this they exemplified the purpose and meaning of the divine work of mercy to all. They both lived the teaching of the Second Vatican Council about all people being called to holiness. They dedicated themselves entirely to Mary, whom they sought to imitate in her role as the Mother of the Church symbolized at the marriage feast of Cana in Galilee when at her suggestion the Lord provided the first of the signs of God's banquet of communion, the Eucharistic wine of hope and joy for all present (cf. Jn 2:1-11).

For John Paul II, Mary is "the woman of the Eucharist."[394] His motto as pope was *"Totus Tuus"* – words which refer to the complete dedication of himself and his service to the Blessed Virgin Mary, whom he calls "the Mother of Hope" in his Last Testament. He explained:

> [T]his phrase is not only an expression of piety, or simply an expression of devotion. It is more. During the Second World War, while I was employed as a factory worker, I came to be attracted to Marian devotion. At first, it had seemed to me that I should distance myself a bit from the Marian devotion of my childhood, in order to focus more on Christ. Thanks to Saint Louis of Montfort, I came to understand that true *devotion to the Mother of God is actually Christocentric; indeed, it is very profoundly rooted in the Mystery of the Blessed Trinity,* and the mysteries of the Incarnation and Redemption.[395]

At the Second Vatican Council the young bishop of Krakow intervened suggesting that the chapter on Mary should be placed after the first chapter on the Church's mystery, not at the end of the document as a kind of appendix.[396]

Mother Teresa, who had begun her journey in religious life by going to Dublin to enter the Loreto Sisters, expressed her devotion to Mary in the following prayer that she wrote:

> Mary my dearest Mother, give me your heart, so beautiful, so pure, so immaculate, so full of love and humility – that I may receive Jesus as you did and go in haste to give him to others.

On September 5, 1997, the day on which she died, Mother Teresa wrote in a general letter:

> Stand near Our Lady to listen to the thirst of Jesus and to answer with your whole heart.[397]

In explaining the Constitutions of the religious congregation she founded, the Missionaries of Charity, Mother Teresa, pointed out to her sisters that they would carry out their mission to slake Jesus' anguished cry on the Cross by remaining close to Mary, who first heard her Son's words "I thirst":

> Let us always remain with Mary our Mother on Calvary near the crucified Jesus, with our chalice made of the four vows, and fill it with the love of self-sacrifice, or pure love, always held up close to His suffering Heart, so that He may be pleased to accept our love.[398]

No less ardently did Pope John Paul II appeal in a Lenten Message to Christians to heed the Savior's thirst by showing solidarity for members of his Mystical Body in the expanding desert places of the world:

Listen to the voice of Jesus who, tired and thirsty, says to the Samaritan woman at Jacob's well: "Give me a drink" (Jn 4:7). Look upon Jesus nailed to the Cross, dying, and listen to his faint voice: "I thirst" (Jn 19:28). Today, Christ repeats his request and relives the torments of his Passion in the poorest of our brothers and sisters…

Call to mind, then, the Lord's words: "Whoever gives to one of these little ones even a cup of cold water because he is a disciple, truly I say to you, he shall not lose his reward" (Mt 10:42). Take to heart and find hope in these other words: "Come blessed of my Father… for I was thirsty and you gave me to drink" (Mt 25:34-35).

During Lent of 1993, in order to practice in a concrete way the solidarity and fraternal charity associated with the spiritual quest of this special season of the year, I ask the members of the Church to remember particularly the men and women suffering the tragic desertification of their lands, and those who in too many parts of the world are lacking that basic yet vital good which is water.[399]

His lifelong message remained unchanged about challenging and encouraging people to become united in entrusting themselves to Christ, in whom, as he had strikingly put it in his first Encyclical Letter, the revelation of love and mercy in human history "has taken on a form and a name: that of Jesus Christ."[400] Thus, nearing the end of his life he had the following words in his homily at a Roman parish:

Hope does not disappoint us, because God's love has been poured into our hearts through the Holy Spirit who has been given to us (Rm 5:5).

The words of the Apostle Paul in the second reading refer to the gift of the Spirit, symbolized by the living water that Jesus promises to the Samaritan woman. The

Spirit is the "pledge" of the definitive salvation that God has promised to us. Man cannot live without hope. Many hopes go down when they crash against the rocks of life. However Christian hope "does not disappoint" because it is based on the solid foundation of faith in the love of God revealed in Christ.[401]

Most appropriately, therefore, the date for the proclamation of the beatification of John Paul II in 2011 was the Feast of Divine Mercy that he had inaugurated to be liturgically celebrated on the Sunday after Easter.[402] He, in fact, died in 2005 on the eve of this day that was so very important to him as characterizing the Church's essential mission of reconciliation and at-onement.

No less fittingly, on World Mission Sunday, October 19, 2003, John Paul II proclaimed that great Missionary of Charity, Mother Teresa as among the Blessed. In his homily he said that she showed in our times

> the way to evangelical "greatness"... the way walked by Christ himself that took him to the Cross: a journey of love and service that overturns all human logic. To be the servant of all!

Because of this attitude, he went on to say:

> Mother Teresa, an icon of the Good Samaritan, went everywhere to serve Christ in the poorest of the poor. Not even conflict and war could stand in her way.[403]

Hope – a new "Beatitude" of sacramental mysticism

This pope and this woman practiced in an exceptional manner the divine truth of Jesus' Gospel summed up in the Beatitudes, among which that of mercy towards humankind is a concrete application of their spiritual understanding that hope is the precious and indispensable fruit of the divine work of mercy. This hope can be thus regarded as a new and refreshing "beatitude" flowing directly from the Savior's heart. Its realization finds expression in the corporal and spiritual works of mercy, the social implications of the Eucharistic Mystery of Christ's Pasch that, as the Church's pastoral solicitude teaches, must be both interiorized personally and exercised in solidarity with others.[404]

The lives of John Paul II and Mother Teresa can be seen as participating in what Pope Benedict XVI called that "sacramental 'mysticism'" which, he went on to explain profoundly,

> is social in character, for in sacramental communion I become one with the Lord, like all the other communicants. As Saint Paul says, "Because there is one bread, we who are many are one body, for we all partake of the one bread" (1 Cor 10:17). Union with Christ is also union with all those to whom he gives himself. I cannot possess Christ just for myself; I can belong to him only in union with all those who have become, or who will become, his own. Communion draws me out of myself towards him, and thus also towards unity with all Christians. We become "one body," completely joined in a single existence. Love of God and love of neighbor are now truly united: God incarnate draws us all to himself. We can thus understand how *agape* also became a term for the Eucharist: there God's own *agape* comes to us bodily, in order to continue his work in us and through us. Only by keeping in mind this Christological and sacramental basis can we correctly understand Jesus' teaching on love.[405]

The undaunted social commitment of both Mother Teresa and John Paul II extended to all humankind the divine Eucharistic *agape*, from which they realized that the Church draws its life. As this pope put it in his last Encyclical Letter, the Eucharistic *agape* contains an "eschatological tension… [that] spurs us on our journey through history and plants a seed of living hope in our daily commitment to the work before us." It brings into an ever clearer focus the perspective of "the Christian vision" that "leads to the expectation of 'new heavens' and 'a new earth' (Rv 21:1)."[406]

This is the significance of the invitation at every Eucharistic Celebration to the Table of Communion: "Blessed are those who are called to his supper." The supper referred to is not only that shared by Christians here and now at a ritual meal, but it also prophetically signifies the hope of participating in the Marriage Feast of the Lamb (cf. Rv 19:7). In view of this Banquet, "full and active participation in the liturgy" – as encouraged by the Second Vatican Council – concerns becoming awakened through everyone taking part in the sacred rites of the Mass to the hope-impelling prospect of sharing fully in the liturgy of heaven. This is the sense of the words: "You have come to Mount Zion and to the city of the living God, the heavenly Jerusalem… and to Jesus, the mediator of a new covenant" (Heb 12:22, 24). Liturgical participation, moreover, cannot be separated from taking an active part and being engaged fully in the community's life of charity, a life that carries out the truth celebrated and contemplated at the twofold table of the Word and Sacrament in deeds serving the needs of people in the world. This gives Christian hope expressed in the Eucharist – "the pledge of future glory" – credibility. The Eucharistic community thus witnesses to the new "beatitude" that Mary, the Mother of the Church, exemplified par excellence: "Blessed… are those who hear the word of God and keep it" (Lk 11:28).

Pope John Paul II, therefore, stated forcefully as pertinent to the pervasive atmosphere of discouragement and despair at the beginning of the new millennium that the expectation in hope

> increases, rather than lessens, our sense of responsibility
> for the world today… so that Christians will feel more
> obliged than ever not to neglect their duties as citizens of
> this world. Theirs is the task of contributing with the light

of the Gospel to the building of a more human world, a world fully in harmony with God's plan. Many problems darken the horizon of our time. We need but think of the urgent need to work for peace, to base relationships between peoples on solid premises of justice and solidarity, and to defend human life from conception to its natural end. And what should we say of the thousand inconsistencies of a "globalized" world where the weakest, the most powerless and the poorest appear to have so little hope! It is in this world that Christian hope must shine forth! For this reason too, the Lord wished to remain with us in the Eucharist, making his presence in meal and sacrifice the promise of a humanity renewed by his love. Significantly, in their account of the Last Supper, the Synoptics recount the institution of the Eucharist, while the Gospel of John relates, as a way of bringing out its profound meaning, the account of the "washing of the feet", in which Jesus appears as the teacher of communion and of service (cf. Jn 13:1-20).[407]

Communion in service (*diakonia*) is at the core of the teaching of the Second Vatican Council which could be regarded as that occasion especially when Wojtyła, a hitherto unknown young bishop, became launched onto the world stage. His prowess and theological insights became recognized by his fellow bishops at this Council in matters pertaining to a deepened and widened approach to human relations, the Church's social doctrine. He contributed particularly to the shaping of the major documents issuing from the Council: on that treating the nature of the Church's mystery, *Lumen Gentium*, and that concerning the Church's relation to the modern world, *Gaudium et Spes*. His hand is also evident in the important declaration, *Nostra Aetate*, which prepared the way to ongoing dialogue with the great non-Christian world religions, Hinduism and Buddhism, and particularly Judaism and Islam. While not leaving the path open for syncretism or relativism nor eclipsing the nature of the Christian Church's mission to be like a sacrament pointing to Christ the Light of the Nations,[408] this declaration contains the following groundbreaking statement:

> The Catholic Church rejects nothing that is true and holy in these religions. She regards with sincere reverence those ways of conduct and of life, those precepts and teachings which, though differing in many aspects from the ones she holds and sets forth, nonetheless often reflect a ray of that Truth which enlightens all men.[409]

The declaration closes with words denouncing any kind of discrimination between people because of race, color, condition of life or religion, urging that

> We cannot truly call on God, the Father of all, if we refuse to treat in a brotherly way any man, created as he is in the image of God. Man's relation to God the Father and his relation to men his brothers are so linked together that Scripture says: "He who does not love does not know God" (1 John 4:8).[410]

This is the message of hope that later as Pope Karol Wojtyła would journey across the world to proclaim. It is the same message that Mother Teresa thoroughly understood and inspired others to live in the communion of love's humble service.

Hope – life in abundance

Both these persons were witnesses to hope insofar as their hearts yearned to share Jesus' thirst, his desire to give all people a deeper sense of life in abundance (cf. Jn 10:10). Against the delusive currents and pressure-groups of these times, which have been described as a "culture of death," they were protagonists who encouraged a genuine appreciation of the significance and value of human life from the first moment of conception to its very end.

Mother Teresa was well-known in supporting the "pro-life" movement. Invited as the guest speaker at the National Prayer Breakfast in Washington on February 3, 1994, the frail woman spoke out courageously in the presence of President Bill Clinton, whose government was known for favoring measures to permit abortion. Beginning by inviting all to join in the prayer attributed to St. Francis of Assisi ("Lord, make me a channel of your peace"), she simply reminded her distinguished audience of various teachings of Jesus and the New Testament about loving God and one's neighbor as the ultimate criterion concerning how we shall be judged. She went on to give examples of the lack of joy in many because of selfishness and a fear to sacrifice – to love till it hurts, as Jesus showed on the Cross. Breakdown in family life and in relations between married persons, she stressed, were the result of putting individual interests first, instead of the priority condition for peace being generosity in the gift of self for others' wellbeing. Busyness about things, material gain or ambition drives a wedge between persons and brings about disquiet and causes many social problems, such as dependency on drugs and the rise of crime. She then poignantly spoke of abortion, which she repeated many times is "the greatest destroyer of peace today." She called abortion "a war against the child, a direct killing of the innocent child, murder by the mother herself." The practical way to overcome this evil destroying society, she stated, was to replace "abortion by adoption" – a way that she had encouraged by contacting clinics, hospitals and police stations. As a result of this she witnessed to the fact that at her children's home in Calcutta over three thousand children had been saved from abortion and, moreover, had brought immense love and joy to their adopting parents. She then went on to speak of the power of giving life being denied and destroyed through contraception as being really a destruction of something important in the lives of spouses, namely, their capacity for being givers of love.

Natural Family Planning is the way that persons turn their attention away from themselves and show consideration for one another. In this memorable speech and on other occasions, such as that when receiving the Nobel Peace Prize in Oslo on December 11, 1979, she had no hesitation before her audiences in speaking movingly about caring for the weakest and most defenseless members in society, the unborn child, the elderly and the suffering, the poor, the neglected and the outcasts, and about helping people to face God's embrace in death with the grace of serenity.

On February 4, 2010, Hilary Rodham Clinton was the guest speaker at the National Prayer Breakfast in Washington. In the course of her address she recalled the powerful effect that Mother Teresa's speech had on her and particularly of their encounter afterwards, when she was struck by how powerful the little sandaled woman's hands were. The now Secretary of State then related that she had felt that she had received an order and a message that was coming "not just through this diminutive woman but from someplace far beyond." The order to set up the Mother Teresa Home for Infant Children in Washington was carried out and Mother Teresa with the glee of a child attended its inauguration the following year.[411]

The cause of defending life – whether of the unborn, destitute or aged – was constantly championed by John Paul II throughout his long pontificate. In his Encyclical Letter on the Gospel of Life, for instance, after citing the words of the Second Vatican Council about the various types of murder – genocide, abortion, euthanasia, or willful self-destruction,[412] he deplored that "this disturbing state of affairs, far from decreasing, is expanding: with the new prospects opened up by scientific and technological progress there arise new forms of attacks on the dignity of the human being." What is even more atrocious, he went on to state, is that "a new cultural climate is developing and taking hold, which gives crimes against life a new and – if possible – even more sinister character, giving rise to further grave concern: broad sectors of public opinion justify certain crimes against life in the name of the rights of individual freedom… and indeed with the free assistance of health-care systems."[413] He also pointed to positive signs of hope, which though sometimes difficult to discern are nevertheless present: many married couples with a sense of responsibility to accept children as God's gift; commitment on the part of researchers to advance medical science to benefit the quality of life; movements and initiatives to raise social awareness about human dignity and its incalculable value; various daily gestures of openness, sacrifice and unselfish care; a gradual shift in public opinion towards a new sensitivity against war and capital punishment; appreciation of the need to care for nature and ecological development. All these lights amid the dark shadows enshrouding the present world situation emanate from the redemptive reality of Christ's blood, which "reveals to man that his greatness, and therefore his vocation, consists in *the sincere gift of self*" so that through participating in it "all draw *the strength to commit themselves to promoting life. It is precisely* this blood that is *the most powerful source of hope; indeed it is the foundation of the absolute certitude that in God's plan life will be victorious.*"[414] Because of participation in the Eucharistic Sacrifice in which Christians sacramentally are cleansed through the new and eternal covenant of Christ's Blood, poured out for the remission of sin, he affirmed:

> The certainty of future immortality and *hope in the promised resurrection* cast new light on the mystery of suffering and death, and fill the believer with an extraordinary capacity to trust fully in the plan of God.[415]

This conviction is repeated later in the following statement about human relatedness in our bodily condition, a theme powerfully proclaimed through this pope's magisterial teaching about God's worthwhile gift of life in abundance, for which the only appropriate response is gratitude as Christians are gathered into the Mystical Body of Eucharistic worship:

> This involves above all proclaiming *the core* of this Gos-

pel. It is the proclamation of a living God who is close to us, who calls us to profound communion with himself and awakens in us the certain hope of eternal life. It is the affirmation of the inseparable connection between the person, his life and his bodiliness. It is the presentation of human life as a life of relationship, a gift of God, the fruit and sign of his love. It is the proclamation that Jesus has a unique relationship with every person, which enables us to see in every human face the face of Christ. It is the call for a "sincere gift of self" as the fullest way to realize our personal freedom.[416]

Crossing the threshold of hope...

John Paul II had a deeply Eucharist-centered, incarnational sense of understanding Christ's Paschal Mystery through which humankind and history itself become embodied in a conversion curve of being re-collected in a dynamic movement towards what St. Paul described as "recapitulation" (cf. Eph 1:10). He explained this notion, which was taken up and developed by St. Irenaeus, the great second-century Father of the Church:

> God's saving plan, "the mystery of his will" (cf. Eph 1:9) for every creature, is described in the Letter to the Ephesians with a distinctive term: to "recapitulate" all things in heaven and on earth in Christ (Eph 1:10). The image could also refer to the roller around which was wrapped the parchment or papyrus scroll of the volumen with a written text: Christ gives a single meaning to all the syllables, words and works of creation and history...
>
> [T]he full realization of the Creator's original plan emerges: that of a creation in which God and man, man and woman, humanity and nature are in harmony, in dialogue and in communion. This plan, upset by sin,

is restored in the most marvelous way by Christ, who mysteriously but effectively carries it out in the present reality, waiting to bring it to fulfillment. Jesus himself said he was the fulcrum and point of convergence of this saving plan when he said: "I, when I am lifted up from the earth, will draw all men to myself" (Jn 12:32). And the Evangelist John presents this work precisely as a kind of recapitulation: "to gather into one the dispersed children of God" (Jn 11:52).[417]

In a poem he expresses this truth:

> I call you and I seek you, oh, Man, in whom
> man's history finds its body.
> I go toward you and not say "come"
> but simply "be."

The poem ends on the note of confident hope about the outcome of the conversion process:

> Through the shadows of history I always reach you
> walking toward each heart, walking toward each thought
> (history – the overcrowding of thoughts, death of hearts).
> I seek your body for all history,
> I seek your depth.[418]

During or in retrospect of a pilgrimage to the Holy Land he wrote:

> Through your body you had a place on earth, the outward
> place of the body you exchanged for a place within, say-
> ing: "Take, all of you, and eat of this."
> The radiation of that place within relates to all the
> outward places on Earth to which I came on pilgrimage.
> You chose this place centuries ago – the place in which
> You give yourself and accept me.[419]

Throughout his journeying in confident faith, despite the deconstructing effects of post-modern rationalism, John Paul II pointed with clarity to Christ – "the splendor of truth," to whom he thus rendered testimony from "the place within" his and every heart:

> But this I know:
> I can't fall apart any further.
> Both the vision and Object entire inhabit
> the very same pit. I speak of it seldom,
> always draw a conclusion instead
> about the world's proper weight
> and my own innate
> depth.[420]

Assent to this light-giving conviction, however, entails descent to terrible depths of darkness, which he knew from personal experience. He spoke on various occasions about how by contemplating Christ's passion as revealing the glory of the mystery of the Trinity we come to perceive all human suffering and darkness becoming a dialogue of love.[421] He recalled the central message of the Spanish mystic St. John of the Cross as being a sure guide for Christians, whose vocation in faith, "the heartbeat of the new evangelization," leads through the dark nights of trial that are illumined by the ardent flame of the Holy Spirit's love to adoration and praise of God. He expressed his desire to share the Castilian saint's message with people "who are living today at this hopeful and challenging hour of history."[422] The teaching of the saint had had a profound influence on John Paul II from the period immediately following the dark days of World War II, when as a student priest in Rome he wrote a doctoral dissertation on the subject of Faith according to St. John of the Cross. This teaching stood him in good stead through his own trials of faith and in his sensitivity to others suffering from violence and terrorism, such as during the Communist regime in Poland or when he endured the assassination attempt on his life in St. Peter's Square on May 13,

1981. While convalescing after this life-imperiling occasion, he wrote an apostolic letter about the redemptive value of the whole span of human suffering: physical, moral and spiritual, illness, plagues of hunger, war, injustice, solitude, the lack of a sense of meaning and purpose in living, the very fragility of human existence, the sorrowful knowledge of sin, the seeming absence of God. All these situations, he pointed out, can be for those who believe and hope in the power of Christ's Cross purifying experiences which might be called the night of faith.

Mother Teresa was so admired as a person radiant with the joy of the Gospel, a model of fulfillment in living a dedicated religious life, someone who inspired hope in others to find true happiness in doing "something beautiful for God," as the journalist Malcolm Muggeridge described her mission. After encountering this woman, he observed: "Something of God's universal love has rubbed off... giving her homely features a noticeable luminosity; a shining quality."[423] Yet, as revealed only to her spiritual superiors in her personal letters, which surprised the world when they were published, for many years she had been plunged in the terrible crucible of spiritual darkness. She wanted to be known as "the saint of darkness," as she put it in a letter:

> If I ever become a Saint – I will surely be one of "darkness." I will continually be absent from Heaven – to light the light of those in darkness on earth.[424]

These words indicate how she understood and fulfilled the mission she received from the Lord, who asked her: "Come be My Light."[425] Her first mention of this state of spiritual destitution and abandonment by God is in a letter going back to the time before she heard on September 10, 1946, while on a train to Darjeeling that "'call within a call' to satiate the thirst of Jesus by serving Him in the poorest of the poor"[426] – that is, while she was still a member of the Institute of the Blessed Virgin Mary (the Loreto Sisters):

Do not think that my spiritual life is strewn with roses
– that is the flower which I hardly ever find on my way.
Quite the contrary, I have more often as my companion
"darkness." And when the night becomes very thick – and
it seems to me as if I will end up in hell – then I simply
offer myself to Jesus. If He wants me to go there – I am
ready – but only under the condition that it really makes
Him happy.[427]

In a letter many years later she spoke of having "since 49 or 50 this
terrible sense of loss – this untold darkness – this loneliness – this
continual longing for God – which gives me that pain deep down
in my heart... The place of God in my soul is blank. – There is no
God in me."[428] This was an anguished cry wrung from the heart of
a person who regarded her life as being merely an "instrument" – "a
pencil in God's hand." Her concern, as she taught her fellow sisters,
was always for "God's work and not our work; that is why we must
do it well. How often we spoil God's work and try to get the glory for
ourselves."[429] She feared getting in the way of the divine design. This
implied that she realized deeply that to be concerned about oneself,
to judge oneself or others, is the greatest presumption, namely, to
live a lie, to steal from the Lord his unique role of being the one who
"will come to judge the living and the dead" – as professed in the
Creed. Despite experiencing prolonged interior spiritual torment, she
never lost her trust and persevered in the purgation of naked faith,
not slackening in "the beautiful hope of seeing Jesus one day."[430] Her
soul-tearing tension consisted in desiring ardently to see him face
to face who is perceived only in a glass darkly in the "distressing
disguise of the poorest of the poor, the unwanted" (cf. 1 Cor 13:12),
to enjoy the fulfillment of God's promises held in the hope he has
implanted in the human heart, in a word, to realize

> what no eye has seen, nor ear heard, nor the heart of man
> conceived, what God has prepared for those who love
> him (1 Cor 2:9).

All human beings are called to be united in communion by "crossing the threshold of hope," as John Paul II poetically described the mystery of journeying in the dynamism of Christ's Passover. In his parable of the woman and the onion, Dostoevsky described the drama of the fact that no one goes to heaven alone. Faithful to the Orthodox and Catholic tradition, he shows that hope must never be focused on individualistic selfish gain, but is a matter of communal salvation. The nature of Christian hope, thus, involves a holistic sense of communion. Anything less than this makes the angels weep for pity, as the wicked woman's guardian does when she falls headlong to hell because she kicks away other persons who cling to her. For the angels share God's hope for all to be saved in the communion of saints.[431]

One of the most memorably moving images, which millions of people were united in beholding on TV screens the world over on April 8, 2005, is that of the pages of a book fluttering about this way and that as they were blown by the playful gusts of the wind. The book was that of the Gospels lying on the coffin of a man whose life witnessed to the challenge, joy and hope that fill the human heart inspired by the breath of the Spirit blowing where he wills. The man was Karol Wojtyła, Pope John Paul II, who throughout his whole life and endeavor recognized that the genuine validity and genius of Christianity finds its clearest expression in the holiness of the lives of the women and men who are the saints. He perceived clearly that the hearts of the saints are "captured by One Heart, by that one heart simplest and gentlest of all."[432] The Heart to which this pope constantly pointed is none other than that of Jesus Christ, from whose pierced side flowed the true depths of meaning and transcendent sense of direction of all human existence. John Paul II's heart, like that of Mother Teresa, was inspired and sustained by the essential rhythm of Christ's revelation of the divine mystery of love for the world. This mystery empowered and impelled them both from their earliest days unto those of their last faltering steps to offer their fellow travelers along humankind's paschal journey a powerful *witness to hope*.[433]

Their lives challenged all people of our times to overcome fear of the future by hope to believe in God's love – that God-etched aspiration of hope which is "to human consciousness what breathing is to the living organism."[434]

Ultimately humankind's journey is homeward towards the New Jerusalem, to which our wandering in this valley of tears leads in the hope of being eternally at-one. It is to this home, the heartland of hope, that our gaze is directed in yearning to contemplate and enjoy the companionship of all those "who have gone before us marked with the sign of faith" in the certain hope of being welcomed in the embrace of "the spouse... Christ and his mother and all his hallows."[435] The focus of Christian hope is to feast at the Nuptial Banquet of the Lamb in sharing fully the Bread of Life that we are now privileged to share in sacred sign.

During his homily on May 1, 2011, at the Eucharistic Celebration at which he declared Karol Wojtyła among the partakers of this heavenly banquet, Pope Benedict XVI summed up his great predecessor's message:

> This was his message: man is the way of the Church, and Christ is the way of man. With this message, which is the great legacy of the Second Vatican Council and of its "helmsman," the Servant of God Pope Paul VI, John Paul II led the People of God across the threshold of the Third Millennium, which thanks to Christ he was able to call "the threshold of hope." Throughout the long journey of preparation for the great Jubilee he directed Christianity once again to the future, the future of God, which transcends history while nonetheless directly affecting it. He rightly reclaimed for Christianity that impulse of hope which had in some sense faltered before Marxism and the ideology of progress. He restored to Christianity its true face as a religion of hope, to be lived in history in an "Advent" spirit, in a personal and communitarian exis-

tence directed to Christ, the fullness of humanity and the fulfillment of all our longings for justice and peace.[436]

By crossing the threshold of hope all people can reach and enter that portal which Charles Péguy describes in his poem, to which reference is repeatedly made in this book about the Paschal spirituality of those persons whose search led deeply into God. These persons are exemplary to all, for they were inspired and sustained by the reality of Christ's Pasch that sets hearts aflame with hope for communion. Péguy expressed the prayer that

> there will be others, great God there will be others,
> One must hope,
> Who already know the taste for bread and who will know how
> to bite into
> a good crust of bread.
> Who will eat heartily.
> Their daily bread.
> Who will eat heartily their daily bread and their eternal bread.[437]

A hunger for this eternal Bread is indeed a hunger for hope, which is ultimately for communion with Christ and with one another. This communion continues to be the focus today, as highlighted at the 50th International Eucharistic Congress at Dublin in 2012. The official prayer for this Congress weaves various threads of spirituality into a rich tapestry of faith-based hope, as affirmed in its second stanza:

> Lord Jesus…
> May your Holy Spirit inflame our hearts,
> enliven our hope and open our minds,
> so that together with our sisters and brothers in faith
> we may recognize you in the Scriptures

and in the breaking of bread.
May your Holy Spirit transform us into one body
and lead us to walk humbly on the earth,
in justice and love,
as witnesses of your resurrection.[438]

Notes

ⁱ *Devotions Upon Emergent Occasions*, 1624. Section 7: "For whom the bell tolls."

ⁱⁱ Disc. 5 "Saintliness, the Standard of Christian Principle" in *Discourses to Mixed Congregations* (London: Longmans, Green and Co., 1906), pp. 98f.

ⁱⁱⁱ *New Seeds of Contemplation* (New York: New Directions, 1972), pp. 59f., cited by Rosemary Haughton, "The Youngest Son," in *Tales from Eternity* (London: George Allen & Unwin Ltd., 1973), p. 49.

1. SpS, n. 49.

2. *The Portal of the Mystery of Hope* [ET] (London/New York: Continuum, 2005); [originally Grand Rapids, MI: Wm. B. Eerdmans Publishing Co., 1996], p. 1.

3. "On Hope" in *Faith Hope Love* [ET] (San Francisco, CA: Ignatius Press, 1997), p. 110.

4. "And the Greatest of These is Hope" in *The Cresset*, May-June 1966; online: www.valpo.edu/cresset/Pelikan/Pelikan_Greatest%20of%20These%20is%20Hope.pdf

5. This phrase is the subtitle of his book *Real Presences* (London: Faber and Faber, 1989).

6. Ibid., p. 202.

7. Even some Christians in recent times have uncritically been drawn into the trend that is described as a "cooling of memories" instead of being rejuvenated in hope through rediscovering their rich heritage of celebrating the "hot memory" of God's commitment to the world manifest in the Paschal Mystery of Christ's life, death and Resurrection. Cf. Miroslav Volf, and William Katerberg, "Introduction: Retrieving Hope" in *The Future of Hope: Christian Tradition amid Modernity and Postmodernity* (Grand Rapids, MI: Wm. B. Eerdmans, 2004), pp. Xf.

8. Pelikan, loc. cit. Pope Benedict XVI discusses at length this rationalistic "faith in progress" as the new form of human hope, which has displaced and brought about a devaluation growth in faith, the path to genuine spiritual wholeness. See SpS, nn. 17ff.

9. See Immanuel Kant's famous essay *An Answer to the Question: What is Enlightenment?* (published in a Berlin monthly periodical *Berlinische Monatscrift*, 4 [1784], pp. 481-94). The debate on the nature of Enlightenment took place in German philosophical and literary circles in the 18th century. See the translation of various essays in *What is Enlightenment? Eighteenth-Century Answers and Twentieth-Century Questions* (Los Angeles/London: The California University Press, 1996). The phrase "Dare to know" (*sapere aude*) is traceable to Horace's letter to his friend Maximus Lollius (*Epistle* I.2.40), whom he exhorts to study and develop his mind instead of frivolously indulging in idleness and pleasure-seeking. See Robert C. Bartlett, *The Idea of Enlightenment: A Post-mortem Study* (University of Toronto Press Incorporated, 2001).

10. Stratford Caldecott argues powerfully and persuasively for the reinstatement of the liberal arts and calls for a serious rethinking of the whole process of education, the thrust of which erstwhile focused through faith on the pursuit of truth and wisdom has been displaced in the modern world's shift towards a thinner and less substantial concentration of interest on rational and scientific methodology, at the cost of sacrificing an integral and transcendent perspective of the significance

and beauty of the liturgical nature of the cosmos. See *Beauty for Truth's Sake: On the Re-enchantment of Education* (Grand Rapids, MI: Brazos Press, 2009). See also Don Cupitt, *The Sea of Faith: Christianity in Change* (London: BBC, 1984), especially pp. 22ff.

11 Cf. Rowan Williams, *Dostoevsky: Language, Faith, and Fiction* (Waco, TX: Baylor University Press, 2008), p. 15. [Italics in the text.] Williams quotes the Russian writer who said he would choose to remain steadfast in believing in Christ even if it were proved that truth lay apart from him. Henri de Lubac, S.J. quotes his famous words: "it is not like a child that I believe in Christ and confess Him. My hosanna has come forth from the crucible of doubt," *The Drama of Atheist Humanism* [ET] (London: Sheed & Ward, 1949), p. 180.

12 *An Essay on the Development of Christian Doctrine* (London: Longmans, Green, and Co., 1909), Introduction, p. 6. Similar statements are found throughout the argument of this work, cf. ibid., Ch. II, Sect. II, 8, p. 82.

13 This phrase in Alfred Lord Tennyson's *In Memoriam* is sometimes employed to describe the attitude of some persons (e.g. George Eliot or William James) whose crisis of faith led them openly and in honesty to reject paying lip service to orthodox Christian beliefs and to throw over the religious practice that they found intellectually unacceptable, formalistic and stuffy. See Timothy Larsen's provocative study, *Crisis of Doubt: Honest Faith in the Nineteenth Century* (OUP, 2006). Tennyson's expressions of doubt, albeit disguised at times, are not untypical of the skeptical spirit of the post-Enlightenment period, which challenged the starchy religious attitudes, traditional values and shallow hypocritical lifestyles of some of his contemporaries. See T.S. Eliot's essay "In Memoriam" (1936) in *Points of View* (London: Faber and Faber, 1951; 5th impression), p. 93. In Tennyson's poem *In Memoriam*, as Dr. Angela Leighton says, his achievement was that he gambled with Darwinian evolutionary theory and the atheism of Lucretius (his favorite pagan Latin poet), but somehow managed to maintain "the gift and insight of Christianity itself: not the quality of faith, but the quality of doubt" – a quality requiring the expulsion of every falsely escapist or hypocritical adherence to the truths of revelation in a complacent and arrogant formalistic kind of religion. See sermon on November 2, 2008, Trinity College Chapel, Cambridge: "God in the Nineteenth Century: Tennyson." Online: www.trin.cam.ac.uk/show.php?dowid= 629.

14 Concerning doubt and searching, see *Pensées* [ET] (Penguin Classics, 1970), pp. 156, 160, 314 [Brunschvicg ed., nn. 194; 553].

15 Cf. *Christian Reflections* (London: Geoffrey Bles, 1967).

16 Cf. e.g., 1 Cor 15:49; Rm 8:29; Col 3:10; 2 Cor 5:14ff.; Ph 2:5-11; Rm 12:1-2; Eph 4:23; 1 Cor 13:1ff.

17 SC, n. 47, citing the words of St. Augustine, *In Joh. Ev.*, Tr. XXVI, n. 13, and the *Magnificat Antiphon* for the Solemnity of Corpus Christi (attributed to St. Thomas Aquinas). In a thorough study Paul Vu Chi Hy, S.S.S., presented the approaches of various philosophers and theologians who in recent years have shown the intrinsic connection between hope and the Eucharist, a connection that in the past didn't receive the attention it merits. See doctoral dissertation for the Australian Catholic University, Fitzroy, Vic., Australia, Mar. 17, 2004: *The Pledge of Future Glory: The Eschatological Dimension of the Eucharist: A Systematic Exploration*. Online: http://dlibrary.acu.edu.au/digitalthe-ses/public/adt-acuvp58.29082005/01front. pdf

18 This point is repeatedly emphasized by Pope Benedict XVI; e.g., in SCar, nn. 70,

94. Cf. also, Joseph Ratzinger, *The Spirit of the Liturgy* [ET] (San Francisco, CA: Ignatius Press, 2000), pp. 45ff., 50, 58.

19 From *God, Christ and the World: A Study in Contemporary Theology* (1969), cited in *Glory Descending: Michael Ramsey and His Writings* (Grand Rapids, MI/ Cambridge, UK: William B. Eerdmans Publishing Co., 2005), p. 132. In passing it may be noted that this outlook is quite different to what is implied in the "message" of John Lennon, referred to above.

20 From the poem "The Second Coming," which was written in 1919 after Yeats had witnessed the havoc wreaked by World War I.

21 *The Eucharist: Communion with Christ and with One Another: Theological and Pastoral Reflections in Preparation for the 50th International Eucharistic Congress, June 10-17, 2012*, nn. 16, 17 (Dublin: Veritas Publications, 2011), pp. 11f. Cf. Tertullian, *Apol.*, XXXIX.

22 *A Song for St. Cecilia's Day, 1687*, lines 11-15.

23 Cf. Joseph Gelineau, S.J., "The Church responds to God with the Word of God" in *The Liturgy and the Word of God* (Collegeville, MN: Liturgical Press, 1959), pp. 84ff.

24 Cf. C. Spicq, O.P., *St. Paul and Christian Living* [ET] (Dublin: Gill and Son, 1964), p. 42, reference to *Contra Arianos*, III.34.

25 Cf. M. Gaudoin-Parker, "The Saving Beauty of the Word," Part I in *Emmanuel Magazine*, Vol. 114 (2008), n. 5, pp. 407ff.; "The Saving Beauty of the Word," Part II in ibid., n. 6, pp. 525ff.

26 *Ep. ad Eph.*, 15 [ET by Maxwell Staniforth] *Early Christian Writings: The Apostolic Fathers* (Penguin Books, 1968), p. 80. Cf. also his *Ep. ad Rm.*, 2.

27 *Essay on Man*, Epistle i, lines 95-96.

28 Cf. e.g., the *Pastoral Constitution on the Church in the Modern World*, which is significantly entitled "The Joys and Hopes," *GS*, nn. 32, 34, 39.

29 Cf. Karl Rahner, S.J., "The Church of the Saints" in *Theological Investigations*, Vol. III [ET] (Baltimore/London: Helicon Press/DLT, 1967), pp. 91ff.

30 *Pensées*, op. cit., p. 312 [Brunschvicq ed., n. 540].

31 Cited by Ian Ker in *John Henry Newman: A Biography* (Oxford/New York: OUP, 2009, first publ. 1988), p. 483.

32 See the Congregation of the Blessed Sacrament, *Rule of Life*, n. 2 "The Founder."

33 Pope Benedict XVI, SpS, n. 2.

34 *God in the Dock*, edited by Walter Hooper (Grand Rapids, MI: Eerdmans, 1970), "The Trouble With 'X'..." (1948), pp. 152-153.

35 Letter to his brother and sister George and Georgina, Friday Mar. 19, 1819, *Selected Poems and Letters of John Keats*, ed. Robert Gittings (Heinemann, 1970), p. 112.

36 Address to women of the Third Order of Mary on June 16, 1855.

37 *The Portal of the Mystery of Hope*, op. cit., p. 68.

38 See Joseph Ratzinger, *The Spirit of the Liturgy*, op. cit., p. 118.

39 SpS, n. 49.

40 200th Anniversary of the birth of St. Peter-Julian Eymard.

41 Parochial Sermon preached after 1856 (PG 280,4), later published in the review *Le*

Très-Saint Sacrement, 16th year (1892), p. 6. Unless otherwise indicated, references to Eymard's writings are from the Internet Site: www.eymard.org. This integral critical edition of Eymard's complete writings in French gives access to the riches of the thought and heritage of this spiritual master. It became available on Dec. 5, 2006 as the lasting contribution of the Generalate of Father Fiorenzo Salvi, S.S.S., through the collaboration and technical expertise of a team at the Benedictine Abbey of Maredsous. All texts in this edition have also been published in seventeen handsomely bound volumes running into some 11,000 pages. See *Pierre-Julien Eymard (1811-1868), Œuvres Complètes* (Centro Eucaristia & Nouvelle Cité, 2008).

[42] *De la douleur, Précédé des Temps Présents* (Lyon, 1849), p. v.

[43] Seymat, *Eucharistia, Passione di una Vita* [Ital. Tr.] (Ponteranica: Centro Eucaristico 2006), p. 23. This testimony was written at the suggestion made by Madame Nathalie Jordan four weeks after Eymard's death (Aug. 1, 1868) and published in *Le Mémorial Catholique*, Jan.-Feb. 1869.

[44] Lewis, *Mere Christianity* (Collins Fontana, 1972), pp. 187f.

[45] SCar, n. 31.

[46] Words from the homily at his canonization, Dec. 9, 1962.

[47] Cf. SCar, n. 94.

[48] Cf. "Statistics Concerning Perpetual Adoration in France in the 19th Century," in Donald Cave, S.S.S., *Eymard, The Years 1845-1851: A Critical Study of the Origins of the Eucharistic Vocation of St. Pierre-Julien Eymard* (Rome: PUG, 1969), Appendix 16C, pp. CLXXVIff.

[49] See André Guitton, S.S.S., *Peter-Julian Eymard 1811-1868: Apostle of the Eucharist* [ET] (Ponteranica, Italy: Centro Eucaristico, 1996). This splendid biography has among its other many merits the particular feature of drawing extensively on Eymard's correspondence.

[50] This has been brought out by Donald Cave, S.S.S., cf. *The "Writings" of St. Peter Julian Eymard 1811-1868*, Melbourne: Blessed Sacrament Fathers (Collection: Studies on the Origins of the Congregation of the Blessed Sacrament, Vol. VI), 1999.

[51] See the letter to Madame Jordan on Mar. 24, 1850 from Chalon-sur-Saône where he was giving an Easter retreat, spending much time preaching or hearing confessions (CO 188,1). In a letter to Mlle. Virginie Danion on June 13, 1862, he shared his alarm about the loss of faith among businessmen and about the amount of evil because it was organized, wealthy and powerful (CO 1131,1).

[52] Jean-Claude Courveille had the original vision to set up a group dedicated to the Blessed Virgin Mary for renewal of the Church in the post-Revolution situation, as the Jesuits had done in the post-Reformation era. But Colin emerged as the acknowledged founder of the Marists, cf. Jan Snijders, S.M., *A Piety Able to Cope: Jean-Claude Colin and the Marist Missions in Oceania* (2008, 2nd ed.). Online: www.mariststudies.org/docs/ A_Piety_Able_to_Cope. Commissioned by Colin, Eymard wrote on Feb. 8, 1846 to Federico Salvioni, a professor at the seminary in Milan, about the origins, end, spirit of the Society of Mary (CO 69).

[53] Jessie Munro, *The Story of Suzanne Aubert* (Auckland University Press, Bridget Williams Books, 1996), p. 23.

[54] *Adv. Haer.*, Bk IV,20.7, "gloria enim Dei vivens homo; vita autem hominis visio Dei." In his letter to families *Gratissimam sane* (Feb. 2, 1994), 11, Pope John Paul

II stated that these words spell out the loftiest description of humanity.

55 He cites this phrase from the post-communion prayer of St. Irenaeus' feast in a conference to his brethren on obedience being the way to realize the end of existence (PR 149, 17).

56 This book was written while he came to terms with family tragedy resulting from his father's death and his mother's long illness. See Eymard's letter of gratitude for this, written at Chalon-sur-Saône on Mar. 10, 1850 (CO 183,1).

57 Cf. G. Maton, *Blanc de Saint-Bonnet, philosophe de l'unité spirituelle (1815-1880)* (Lyon-Paris, 1961); Raymond Christoflour: "Blanc de Saint-Bonnet, prophète de la douleur" in *Prophètes du XIXe siècle* (Paris: La Colombe, 1954), pp. 93-121. Cf. also, J. Buche, *L'École mystique de Lyon (1776-1847)* (Paris, 1935).

58 See Lauréat Saint-Pierre, S.S.S., *"L'Heure" du Cénacle dans la Vie et les Œuvres de Pierre-Julien Eymard* (Lyon: Lescuyer, 1968), pp. 175-84, 197-99.

59 Ozanam's association with the parish church of Saint-Nizier is clear from the fact that this is where he was married. Cf. Austin Fagan, *Through the Eye of a Needle: Frédéric Ozanam, Principal Founder of the Society of St. Vincent de Paul* (Slough, UK: St. Paul Publications, 1989). Charles-Alphonse is mentioned in a letter from Lyons to Fr. François-Joseph Morcel, S.M. (Nov. 26, 1845, CO 62,1). Fr. Jean Léon Le Prevost, who was part of the first group of the St. Vincent de Paul Conferences, founded in 1845, the Society of the Brothers of St. Vincent de Paul, to whom Fr. Eymard preached the annual retreat from May 4-9, 1868 (PA 10).

60 See Ozanam, *Poètes franciscains en Italie au XIIIe siècle* (1852). A year later he brought out a great work on the Church's influence in educating the Teutonic tribes: *La Civilisation chrétienne chez les Francs* (1853).

61 A general description of the intellectual climate in Europe is found in Wilfrid Ward's *Life of John Henry Cardinal Newman* (London/New York: Longmans, Green & Co., 1912), Chapter 15: "Liberal Catholicism," pp. 458ff. Cf. also J. Gadille, *La Diocèse de Lyon*, Paris: "La Reconstruction du diocèse après la Révolution (1803-1839)" and "Les Catholiques lyonnais et la question sociale (1831-1871)," 1983.

62 It will be recalled that Karl Marx and Friedrich Engels wrote the *Manifesto of the Communist Party* between Dec. 1847 and Jan. 1848. Its famous opening words indict all European Powers (including the Pope) for trying to exorcise the specter haunting the Continent.

63 Cf. Norman B. Pelletier, S.S.S., *Tomorrow Will Be Too Late: A Life of Saint Peter Julian Eymard* (Cleveland, OH: Emmanuel Publishing, 1992), pp. 52f. In a letter (Apr. 9, 1848, CO 111,2) he reassured his sister Marianne of his safety, expressing surprise that even in the mountainous region of La Mure communism, "which is contrary to reason and good sense," arrived there, but he was confident that God can draw good out of evil.

64 See Snijders, loc. cit., and also Mary Catherine Goulter, *Sons of France: A Forgotten Influence on New Zealand History* (Wellington, 1957).

65 Cf. the *Annales de la Propagation de la Foi* mentioned by Munro, op. cit., p. 21.

66 Written at Belley on July 7, 1844 to the Abbé Bramerel (CO 44, 1) and also in a letter from Lyons on May 16, 1845 to his sisters (CO 55, 1). Father Eymard copied out Father Colin's praise of this martyr at the end of the Marist first General Chapter on Apr. 24, 1842 (cf. NP 3, 5).

67 Letter written at Lyons to Madame Josephine Gourd on Jan. 28, 1848 (CO 99,1). He is reported as exclaiming: "Ah! How I would be glad to go to the foreign mis-

sions, even though I wouldn't be able to do much there, to offer God the complete sacrifice of myself, my country, my relatives, friends, acquaintances, mother tongue, everything I've learnt, and be obliged to begin from scratch new things." E. Troussier, *Le Bienheux Pierre-Julien Eymard*, t. I (Paris, 1928), p. 187.

68 See his personal notes on Aug. 31, 1839 (NR 12,7). [Italics in text.]

69 In a letter from La Seyne-sur-Mer to Raymond de Cuers on June 11, 1855 (CO 508,1) he quoted the words of the Superior General, Fr. Favre, S.M. about being prudent: "you are above all a Marist, the Society is your bark of salvation."

70 Letter to Mlle. Marguerite Guillot, May 18, 1856 (CO 576,1). He makes similar avowals in other correspondence: again to Guillot, May 31, 1856 (CO 582,1); to Joséphine Gourd, May 31, 1856 (CO 583,1); to Fr. Jean-François Denis, S.M., who succeeded him as the Superior of La Seyne-sur-Mer, June 1, 1856 (CO 588,1); to Mr. Crenzet, July 5, 1856 (CO 605,1); to Mr. Clappier, July 8, 1856 (CO 609,1). He told the Perpetual Adorers of the Sacred Heart on Jan. 31, 1861, that to have a "Marist heart" pertains to every Christian (PA 2,3).

71 During his Great Retreat at Rome on Mar. 11, 1865 he meditated on the Blessed Virgin Mary's special care for him (NR 44,94), also, how she had led him by the hand to the priesthood and then to the Eucharist (NR 44,109). Earlier he had stated that Mary is "doubly his good mother" for showing him his "second vocation," cf. letter to Mlle. Stéphanie Gourd, July 1, 1856 (CO 602,1).

72 Apart from his initial attempt to join the Oblates of Mary Immaculate founded in Marseilles by Blessed Charles-Eugène de Mazenod and his many years as a Marist, from childhood to the very end of his life he frequently went on pilgrimage to Marian shrines, La Laus, l'Osier (where he celebrated his first Mass), Fourvière had a special attraction to him. He supported the genuineness of the apparitions of the Virgin at La Salette even despite hesitations about them by the Curé d'Ars, see his letters to Father Rousselot (CO 241, 249, 458). On Sept. 19, 1859, Feast of Our Lady of La Salette, also of the Seven Sorrows of Mary, he blessed the Paris chapel of the Sister Servants, as Marguerite Guillot recalls (PS 73,1). He celebrated his last Mass on July 21, 1868, in the chapel of the Missionaries of La Salette in Grenoble, see Guitton, op. cit., p. 333.

73 This was, according to tradition in the Congregation, on May 1, 1868, while inaugurating the month of Mary at the novitiate of Saint-Maurice, see Guitton, p. 326. In fact, already on July 23, 1858, when explaining the Rule to the Sisters in Paris he had spoken of honoring the Blessed Virgin with this title, cf. PS 52,1. This title was officially approved by Pope St. Pius X on Dec. 30, 1905.

74 This perspective is seen in the Second Vatican Council's Dogmatic Constitution on the Mystery of the Church, *LG*, Ch. 8. Paul VI gave her the new title "Mother of the Church" during the Second Vatican Council, cf. Paul VI, Discourse of 21 Nov. 1964: *AAS* 56 (1964) 1015; and John Paul II stated that she guides the faithful to the Eucharist, cf. RM, n. 44.

75 Letter to Mme. Tholin-Bost, Oct. 22, 1851 (CO 286,1).

76 Feb. 11, 1852 (CO 325,1). Cf. Guitton, op. cit., p. 81, the date is erroneously given as 1851.

77 At the Marian shrine of Laus as a boy Eymard had met this priest, who assured him in his desire to be a priest and also permitted him to receive Holy Communion every Sunday.

78 Aug. 2, 1855 (CO 520, 1).

79 Guitton states that the first of these events recalls an earlier one, Eymard's experi-

ence while assistant priest at Chatte, when at the "Rock of Saint-Romans" the grace he received was more of a general Christological insight than being specifically Eucharistic, though this was perhaps implicit, cf. Guitton, op. cit., pp. 66f.

[80] The date of this second event is not entirely clear due to the fact that in writing to friends he indicates also Jan. 1 and Feb. 2, 1851, cf. Guitton, op. cit., p. 73.

[81] Feb. 3, 1851 (CO 243,1). Cf. Guitton, op. cit., p. 74. In fact this letter was never sent.

[82] He broke this good news to various persons, e.g., to Mlle. Marguerite Guillot, May 18, 1856 (CO 576); to Mme. Tholin-Bost, May 18, 1856 (CO 577); to Mlle. Adèle de Revelde Nesc, May 18, 1856 (CO 578); to his friend the Curé of Ars, Sept. 24, 1856 (CO 626).

[83] Letter of May 1, 1861 (CO 1030,1).

[84] As he stated in a letter on Feb. 18, 1866 (CO 1742) to the Countess de Fraguier, who undertook to collect money to support the project as her sister (Countess d'Andigné) had done.

[85] See, for instance PC 13,1; PC 14,1; PC 15; PC 16,1.

[86] Cf. *Le Très-Saint Sacrement*, Aug. and Nov. 1864 (PG 243 and PG 245). The records indicate that in the course of the twenty-four celebrations between 1859 and 1868, 766 youth (without mention of the number of girls) had received their First Communion, cf. Guitton, op. cit., pp. 294f.

[87] See especially the last of these retreats given to them on June 26-27, 1868 (PC 6).

[88] As he described in drafts of their Statutes (cf. RA 30 to RA 32). See Ephrem Chaignat, S.S.S., "Saint Peter Julian Eymard Among the Workers and the Rag-Pickers"/ "The Work of the First Communion of Adults" in *Ensemble/Together* (Rome: Congregation of the Blessed Sacrament), nn. 29 (Jan. 1979) and 30 (May 1979).

[89] Cf. the decrees of Pope St. Pius X, *Sacra Tridentina Synodus* (Dec. 16, 1905) and *Quam Singulari* (Aug. 8, 1910).

[90] See, for instance, his letter to Madame Lepage on May 20, 1868 (CO 2172,1).

[91] See SC, n. 55.

[92] Cf. PC 13, 2.

[93] Cf. *On Christian Perfection*, Patrologia Graeca 46.254-255.

[94] For instance see: NV 3:26; RT 15,5 (reference to Tertullian); PG 14,9; PG 293,6 etc.

[95] See his unsent letter to Father Colin, Feb. 3, 1851 (CO 243,1); letter to Pius IX, Aug. 2, 1855 (CO 520, 1).

[96] The Abbé Bernard Nodet, *Jean-Marie Vianney, Le Curé d'Ars: Sa pensée – Son coeur* (Paris: éd. Xavier Mappus, Foi Vivante, 1966), p. 98, cited by Pope Benedict XVI in his letter to priests for the inauguration of the Year for Priests [dated June 16, 2009 and published in the June 24 English edition of *L'Osservatore Romano*]; cf. also CCC, n. 1589.

[97] Letter of July 16, 1865 (CO 1593,1).

[98] 1st meditation on the Feast of the Incarnation, Mar. 25, 1865 (NR 44, 129).

[99] Cf. PA 1,54-56. Cf. also his reflections about priests in mortal sin Sept. 15, 1846 (NR 30,5).

[100] He often spoke of the danger of tepidity, cf. Sermon on Feb. 12, 1837 (PG 35,8);

retreat to the Benedictine community of La Pierre-qui-Vire, Oct. 1, 1861 (PA 3,1); annual retreat to religious of Angers, Aug. 28, 1866 (PR 72,11). See also Chapter IV.5 on adoration, in the Constitutions of the Congregation 1864 (RR 78,4). He quotes St. Bonaventure about tepidity being an illness (*De prof. rel.*, c. 78), cf. notes on various topics in Dec.-Jan. 1864, 65 (NP 61,1).

[101] He collaborated with a priest of the Paris clergy, the Abbé Arthur Dhé, in trying to initiate an innovative project to rehabilitate priests in difficulties. The project failed, because the latter didn't follow Father Eymard's instructions, to which he preferred his own ideas. See Eymard's letter to the said Abbé on Nov. 1, 1866 (CO 1865,1). This letter is followed by another asking the blessing of the project by Pope Pius IX, who willingly granted the request (CO 1865,2).

[102] See Troussier, op. cit., t.II, Chap. 32 titled: "Je laisserais tout pour les prêtres."

[103] Cf. e.g., sermon notes in a diary for 1859 (PG 347,1). See also above regarding his appreciation of the patristic teaching on deification or divinization (*theosis*) through Communion.

[104] Cf. PG 164 and PG 165,1-3. Preached before 1856.

[105] May 31, 1868 (PP 61,2). The note in Cave, *The "Writings,"* op. cit., p. 34, n. 33 erroneously gives the date as March 31.

[106] Letter May 25, 1853 (CO 409,1).

[107] See for example his instruction on Jan. 17, 1867 during a Triduum at Nantes (PO 29,3).

[108] See, for instance, one of the many drafts of the Rule of the Congregation before 1863, Chap. 1, 2 (RR 44,2); Novena of the Sacred Heart preached to the Sister Servants in Paris, June 1, 1858 (PS 23,1). Cf. also Triduum preached in Ghent, July 25-28, 1858 (PO 20).

[109] Retreat of Rome, Mar. 29, 1865 (NR 44, 136).

[110] Cf. e.g., letter to the Abbé Bramerel, Apr. 8, 1845 (CO 52,1); Father de Cuers, Sept. 23, 1859 (CO 873, 1); Great Retreat of Rome, Feb. 3, 1865 (NR 44, 19); Chapter XXVII of his 1864 Rule (RR 78, 27); a sermon on the Feast of the Assumption, Aug. 15, before 1856 (PG 211,1); a sermon published in the periodical (that he began) *Le Très-Saint Sacrement*, no. 2 "The Eucharist is Life" (PG 242, 1); preaching during a Triduum on the "Eucharistic Miracle," July 25-29, 1858 (PO 20,17); a sermon on Nov. 1, 1867 (PP 42, 4).

[111] This imagery is present throughout the Scriptures. Particularly in the Gospel parables a distinct tension is expressed between the "already" and "not yet" significance of the kingdom of God/heaven, and regarding its subjects being "in" but not "of" this present world. This is poignantly brought out in Jesus' trial before the relativistic skeptic Roman Governor, Pontius Pilate, to whom he retorts that his kingdom is of a different order of power to that in the common misconception of domination, cf. Jn 18:33ff. See also the Preface for the Feast of Christ the King, Roman Missal, Pr. 51.

[112] As was brought out well at the Second Vatican Council, cf. *LG* and *GS*. In both of these documents the notion of "service" (*diakonia*) is repeatedly highlighted.

[113] Rome Retreat, Feb. 5, 1865 (NR 44,22).

[114] As Jaroslav Pelikan describes this approach in *Christian Doctrine and Modern Culture (since 1700)* (Chicago and London: The University of Chicago Press, 1991), pp. 60f., 118ff. Attention to a proper use of the affections in piety is evident in a book by the 17-18th century French mystic Mme. Guyon (Jeanne Marie Bouvier de

la Motte), *L'âme, amante de son Dieu* [Cologne, 1717; Paris, 1790]. It may perhaps be this book which Eymard had in mind and which he was recommending to Mme. Antoinette de Grandeville in his letter of Oct. 18, 1857 (CO 709,1). His teaching on fostering an intimate relationship with the Lord, however, had nothing to do with the heresy of Quietism associated with Guyon, although some people accused him of this after his death. Cf. Cave, *The "Writings,"* op. cit., pp. 20, 28, 109, 157ff. In fact, he was well aware of the dangers of this erroneous approach in the spiritual life, although in his opinion persons holding it were in good faith; cf. e.g., a letter to M. Emmanuel de Leudeville on May 12, 1859 (CO 824,1); his personal notes on active contemplation (NP 49,5).

[115] Sermon (PG 250,8). It has been conjectured that Father Eymard preached this sermon on the adoration of the Magi at the Church of St. Andrea della Valle in Rome on Jan. 10, 1865, in the octave of the Epiphany while residing at the French seminary during the first part of his long sojourn in Rome from towards the end of 1864 to Mar. 26, 1865.

[116] In St. Thomas Aquinas' famous phrase, which Father Eymard quotes from the Council of Trent about frequent Communion (Session 13, Decree on the Eucharist, Ch. 2) in the 3rd part of his *Vademecum* (1838?) about the means to perseverance, NV 9,58.

[117] Stratford Caldecott draws attention to St. Paul's tripartite anthropology of body, soul, and spirit (*soma/psyche/pneuma*) in 1 Th 5:23, which expresses the ancient Hebrew understanding of being integrally human (*nefesh-ruah-neshamah* – the animal-mental-spiritual aspects) and which is preferable to a Greek dualistic body-soul slant followed for centuries in Western philosophy and theology, cf. *Beauty for Truth's Sake*, op. cit., pp. 141f. A dualistic approach produced the distorted understanding of consciousness as "the ghost in a machine" that Gilbert Ryle brilliantly exposed and refuted. Cf. *The Concept of Mind* (Chicago: University of Chicago Press, 1949).

[118] Cf., e.g., a sermon preached before 1856 (PG 143,4); the Directory on the Servants' Constitutions (Ch. XVI) regarding Communion (RS 12,38-39).

[119] Tesnière's testimony of Eymard's words, cited by Cave, *The "Writings,"* op. cit., p. 239, n. 27.

[120] *The Diary of a Country Priest* [ET] (Collins: Fount, 1979), pp. 19f.

[121] See EE, nn. 5-6, 48.

[122] This teaching is particularly evident in his conferences to the Sister Servants. See, for instance, his opening conference of a retreat to them at Angers, Oct. 17, 1864 (PS 514,3); second meditation of the 3rd day, Oct. 19, 1864 (PS 523,3).

[123] Cf. Notes on making a visit to the Blessed Sacrament, copied by Marguerite Guillot (PD 43,2). See Karl Rahner, S.J. on the meaning and purpose of adoration and visits to the Blessed Sacrament, "On developing Eucharistic Devotion" in *Mission and Grace*, Vol. I [ET] (London/New York: Sheed & Ward, 1963), pp. 276ff.

[124] Conference to the Third Order of Mary on Dec. 28, 1846 (PT 22,1). He refers or cites Sg 2:16 on numerous occasions, e.g., in a sermon at a First Communion (PC 9,1); a sermon on the unique intimacy experienced with the Lord in Eucharistic communion, retreat at Tours on Nov. 21, 1865 (PD 33,2). A study of Eymard's references to the Canticle of Canticles in relation to his Eucharist-oriented understanding of prayer would be most interesting regarding its similarity to the mystical teaching of St. Bernard of Clairvaux on fostering a pure disinterested love that awakens an eschatological desire for the vision of God. This desire cultivated in 12th century

monastic milieu made Solomon's Songs greatly loved, cf. Jean Leclercq, O.S.B., *The Love of Learning and the Desire for God* [ET] (London: SPCK, 1978), pp. 90f.

[125] Conference on prayer in notes taken by Tesnière, Aug. 12, 1867 (PR 114,1).

[126] This method is mentioned in drafts of the Constitutions and also in conferences to the Sister Servants, cf. e.g., retreat at Nemours, Nov. 10, 1866 (PS 620,1); see also a conference to a religious congregation (PA 72). It is also alluded to in his letter to Pope Pius IX, Aug. 2, 1855 (CO 520, 1). Eymard had learned this method taught by St. Leonard of Port Maurice (1676-1751) while a novice with the Oblates of Mary Immaculate, cf. Guitton, op. cit., p. 26. This method develops what St. Thomas Aquinas stated about the four fundamental attitudes of human beings in relation to God, cf. *S.T.*, Ia IIae, q. 102, a. 3, ad 10.

[127] Letter to Virginie Danion on Aug. 24, 1857 (CO 690,1). This woman, who had for some time been a member of a community of Reparatory Adoration founded by Mother Théodelinde Dubouché, left it to pursue her calling to promote perpetual adoration in dioceses and to establish a community of thanksgiving, cf. Guitton, op. cit., p. 290. Cave discusses at length Danion's attraction to Eucharistic thanksgiving and a purely contemplative lifestyle, which caused concern to Mother Dubouché and eventually resulted in her departure; see *Eymard: The Years 1845-1851*, op. cit., ch. XII, pp. 367ff.

[128] From the poem "Christmas," by George Herbert.

[129] This was emphasized at the XIIth Synod of Bishops in 2008 as an ideal way of preparing for the ministry of the Word; see Pope Benedict XVI, Post-Synodal Apostolic Exhortation, VD, nn. 86-87 et passim.

[130] He understood this ministry, as taught by the Jesuits, should be based on the Scriptures and teaching of the Fathers, cf. notes on preaching Jan. 7, 1839 (NV 11,15).

[131] Although it isn't suggested that Eymard had in mind the rich patristic overtones of the phrase "mystic words," nevertheless, the expression echoes St. Augustine's teaching on the consecrating presence of the Holy Spirit working invisibly, cf. *De Trinitate*, III.4.10. St. Justin Martyr states that the "eucharisted food" is transformed "through the word of prayer" (*Apol.* I.66). This expression may be alternatively rendered: "the prayer of the word (or Word)"; or, "prayer to the Word who came from him"; cf. Henry Bettenson, *The Early Christian Fathers* (OUP, 1969), p. 62 n. 3. The N.T. basis of this may be 1 Tm 4:4-5: "Everything created by God is good… if it is received with thanksgiving; for then it is consecrated by the word of God and prayer."

[132] PG 15,9; cf. PG 14,17, texts written in his own hand, preceded by two pages of about 50 quotations from the Scriptures and some from the Fathers.

[133] Cf. the following documents regarding the importance of the two parts of the Mass and the dignity of God's Word: SC, nn. 48 & 51; DV, n. 21; PO, n. 18. See A.M. Roguet, O.P., "The Whole Mass Proclaims the Word of God" in *The Liturgy and the Word of God* [ET] (Collegeville, MN: The Liturgical Press, 1959), pp. 67ff.; cf. also Yves Congar, O.P., "Les deux formes du pain de vie dans l'Evangile et dans la Tradition" in E. Fischer - L. Bouyer (éds.), *Parole de Dieu et sacerdoce* (Tournai: Mélanges J.-J. Weber, 1962), pp. 21-58.

[134] He cites in this regard the words of Origen and Augustine (cf. PG 14. 16 and 18). Origen pointed out that the Word of God requires as much care and reverence as is shown to the Eucharist, cf. *Hom. in Exod.*, 13,3. Other patristic references: Hilary of Poitiers (c.300-c.368), *Tractatus in Ps. 127*, 10; Caesarius of Arles (469-541), *Sermo* 300.

Notes

135 Cf. *Imitation of Christ*, Bk. IV, Ch. XI.4.

136 His preaching as a young Marist wasn't spared the criticism from its Founder, Colin, who frankly upbraided him for being "mediocre," and advised him to prepare his sermons in writing and not rely on ex tempore inspiration. Cf. Cave, *Eymard: The Years 1845-1851*, op. cit., p. 62.

137 From Herbert's poem, "The Flower."

138 Cf. St. John Chrysostom, *Homily 61*. This imagery, linked with the vision of Is 6:6ff., was also employed by other Fathers especially of the Antiochian school of theology and the method of exegesis in Syria. Cf. e.g., Theodore of Mopsuestia, *Hom. bapt.*, V. 36-38; John Damascene (*De Fide Orth.* iv), referred to by St. Thomas Aquinas, *S.T.* III, q.79 art.1, ad.2.

139 This was through the zeal of Mlle. Émilie Tamisier, one of Eymard's spiritual daughters. Cf. Ferdinand Pratzner, S.S.S., "The International Eucharistic Congresses 1881-1989: Origin and Development" in *The International Eucharistic Congresses for a New Evangelization* (Vatican City, 1991), pp. 7ff.

140 Cf. Giuseppe Vassali, S.S.S., "Origin and Development of the Priests' Eucharistic League" [ET], *Adoremus* (periodical published in Britain), Vol. LXVII, No. 1 (1987), pp. 7ff.

141 Members of the Congregation of the Blessed Sacrament, notably Fathers Eugène Couet, Tesnière, and Estévenon, played an important part together with some Jesuits in the controversy at the end of the 19th – beginning of the 20th century about frequent Communion. Cf. Leo Boismenu, S.S.S., "L'Apostolat de la Communion Fréquente" in *Centenaire de la Congrégation du Très Saint Sacrement Analecta*, Vol. IV, Fasc. VII-IX (Rome: Curie Généralice, 1956), pp. 129ff.

142 PG 144,1. This parochial sermon dates from before 1856.

143 PG 283, 1-7, preached after 1856.

144 Cf. PC 18, 2, also preached after 1856. The scriptural texts are juxtaposed in Eymard's sermon notes.

145 Letter to Madame Tholin-Bost, Feb. 11, 1852 (CO 325,1). He mentioned in this letter that adoration was increasing at Toulon and asks her to send him some leaflets to distribute among the sailors and the four thousand convicts, who despite their chains are beautiful souls. This letter was written during a time he was ministering to convicts, whose terrible conditions he compared to hell (cf. PG 48,5).

146 Tenison Woods, *Memoirs*, quoted by Tom Knowles, S.S.S., in the *Newsletter of St. Francis' Church* (Melbourne, Oct. 2010). Through Tenison Woods no doubt Eymard's spirituality was also imbibed by St. Mary MacKillop, whose statue is close to the sanctuary of St. Francis' Church, where her parents were married and she was baptized and confirmed.

147 Address to mothers (?) of the Third Order of Mary on June 16, 1855 (PT 98,4). He employed a similar image in a retreat conference to Servants of the Blessed Sacrament at Angers on Oct. 22, 1864 (PS 561,3): "The holy Virgin is the first attractive figure whom God has placed on our path… A child doesn't run towards his/her father. Our Lord has given us Mary as a mother whom we already know by this name in order to attract us tenderly."

148 Ibid. [Italics in the text.]

149 Cf. Augustine, *In Joh. Ev.*, Tr. I,7; XVIII.1; XX,1; LXI, 4-5; CXIX, 2; *In Joh. Ep.*, Hom. V, 1. See Eymard: preparatory meditation on the first day of a retreat at the end of 1858/beginning of 1859 (PD 19,1); letter to de Cuers Dec. 31, 1862 (CO

137

1197,2); regarding thanksgiving after Communion, Constitutions/Directory of the Sister Servants, 1863 (RS 12,39); regarding being education in love, Notes for sermon (PG 283,7); conference on recollection, Dec. 11, 1866 at Ghent (PD 36,9); retreat to his religious, Aug. 11, 1867 (PR 111,3).

150 Cf. e.g., Clement of Alexandria, *Pedagogue*, I.49.2 and hymn at the end of the *Pedagogue*; Augustine, *In Joh Ev.*, Tr. I, 7; XVIII, 1; XX, 1; Julian of Norwich, *The Revelations of Divine Love*, Chapters 60, 63, 64. The imagery of God nursing human beings is rarely used today in preaching because breast-feeding is a rarity and also a woman's breasts are often seen as a sex symbol; see Edward Engelbrecht, "God's Milk: An Orthodox Confession of the Eucharist" in *Journal of Early Christian Studies* (Winter) Vol. 7, No. 4 (Johns Hopkins University Press, 1999), pp. 509-526. See also, Mike Aquilina, "Nursing Mothers in the Preaching Fathers," Online: www.fathersofthechurch.com/2006/06/24/nursing-mothers-in-the-preaching-fathers.

151 See e.g., sermon plan, July 20, 1862 (PG 240,8); Eucharistic Triduum for Forty Hours at Saint Aignan (Loire-et-Cher), Aug. 22-24, 1862 (PO 23,4).

152 July 16, 1868 (PP 67,2-3).

153 Cf. *Pensées* [ET] op. cit., p. 154 [Brunschvicg ed., nn. 277-8.]

154 Cf. Augustine, *In I Joh. Ep.*, Hom. IV, 6, cited by Pope Benedict XVI, SS, n. 33.

155 To apply to the Eucharist a phrase from Francis Thompson's poem *The Kingdom of God*.

156 In Dylan Thomas' delightful phrase, cf. *Poem in October*.

157 The expression "soul's Bread" owes its inspiration to the title of a chapter, "Beauty, Bread of the Soul," in Thomas R. Nevin, *Simone Weil: Portrait of a Self-exiled Jew* (University of North Carolina Press, 1991), p. 148.

158 See Karl Rahner, S.J., "Priest and Poet" in *Theological Investigations*, Vol. III [ET] (Baltimore/London: Helicon Press/ DLT, 1967), p. 307: "to the priest... has been given the word of God. This makes him a priest... Every other word that he speaks, that he reflects upon, that he theologizes over, that he proclaims, for which he demands faith, for which he is prepared to pour out his blood – every other word is only explanation and echo of this one word. In it the priest, his person wholly absorbed into Christ, says only that which Christ has said. And in it Christ has said only one thing: himself as our gift... If he speaks of the earth, then he cannot forget that he lifts up the fruits of our poor fields and vineyards as a sacrament into the eternity of heaven. If he speaks of man, of his dignity and his depth, he alone can tell the real truth about man – *'Ecce homo!'* – and truly show the flesh of sin, which is laid on the altars of God in sacrifice."

159 To borrow St. Justin Martyr's pregnant phrase, cf. *Apol.* I,66 & 67: "eucharisted" meaning "thanksgiving having been offered," see above note 131.

160 He first alluded to this in a letter from the residence of his friend Blanc de Saint-Bonnet to Father de Cuers on Oct. 26, 1863 (CO 1306,1). The idea would seem to have haunted him for years, for he had cherished a desire to establish Eucharistic centers modeled on the nascent Christian community of the disciples with Mary in the Cenacle; see his letter to Marguerite Guillot on Sept. 20, 1856 (CO 624,1) a letter in which he calls Mary "Our Lady of the Cenacle."

161 Retreat of Rome, 2nd meditation on the anniversary of his baptism, Feb. 5, 1865 (NR 44,22). Mention of Jacob goes back to his early days, cf. e.g., his letter to Madame Perroud in 1842 (CO 26,1); his annual retreat on Sept. 18, 1842 (NR 35,17).

[162] See the excellent analysis of the 1865 Retreat of Rome by Hervé Thibault, S.S.S., *Studies on the Spiritual Journey of Saint Peter Julian Eymard*, Studies on the Origins of the Congregation of the Blessed Sacrament, Vol. IIIA, Rome: Editions of the General House of the Congregation.

[163] He quotes this verse no less than 178 times.

[164] See Gerald O'Collins, S.J., *Second Journey: Spiritual Awareness and the Mid-Life Crisis* (Mahwah, NJ: Paulist Press, 2000).

[165] "Little Gidding" V in *Four Quartets.*

[166] The Feastday of St. Benedict, founder of Western Monasticism, Mar. 21, 1865 (NR 44,119).

[167] Blanc de Saint-Bonnet's idea (quoted at the beginning of this chapter) may well have suggested the vow to him, as Cave argues. It moreover may indeed have helped Eymard to reshape his understanding of what he had assimilated from the so-called French School of Spirituality so that this vow, though modeled on that of M. Jean-Jacques Olier, has certain significant modifications. Cf. Cave, *The "Writings,"* op. cit., pp. 35 n. 43, 222, 230f., 563f. Another source may also have been the teaching on mystical union by Jesuit writer Jean Joseph Surin (1600-1660), cf. Cave, ibid., pp. 231, 247 n. 93. Eymard recommended a book of this author to Mother Marguerite Guillot in a letter on May 18, 1868 (CO 2168,1). On Surin, see Michel de Certeau, *The Mystic Fable*, Vol. I [ET] (The University of Chicago Press, 1995), pp. 179ff.

[168] Eymard refers to St. Ignatius of Antioch's desire to become Christ's pure wheat (*Ep. ad Rom*, 4.1), see his sermon on how Christ the second Adam enables humankind to share his divine nature (1 P 1:4): sermon on Christmas Day 1867 (PP 48,2); also conference to the Sisters on dying to self-love, Nov. 3, 1858 (PS 92,1); letter to Virginie Danion, Jan. 3, 1867 (CO 1895,1). Ignatius had said that his desire would be fulfilled, only through martyrdom in which his eros would be crucified; cf. *Ep. ad Rom.*, 7.2. The post-apostolic Father's phrase was deliberately reinterpreted by Origen to bring out Christ's nuptial union with humankind (*Prol. in Cant.* 3); cf. G.L. Prestige, "Eros: or, Devotion to the Sacred Humanity" in *Fathers and Heretics* (London: SPCK, 1963), pp. 180ff. This total surrender to Christ is also expressed in the famous prayer near the end of the *Spiritual Exercises* (n. 234) of the other Ignatius (of Loyola), a prayer Eymard had long ago made his own. Cf. retreat notes as a Marist on Aug. 30, 1838 (NR 12,6).

[169] On Eymard's key insight about the gift of self in imitation of the Eucharist see Manuel Barbiero, S.S.S., *Vita Eucharistica e Vita Religiosa in S. Pierre-Julien Eymard (1811-1868)* (Verona: PUG, 1991); [ET] *Eucharist Life and Religious Life in St. Peter Julian Eymard (1811-1868)*, photocopy, New York, 1991.

[170] Cf. Teresa of Avila, *Autobiography*, Ch. 23.

[171] Conference during their annual retreat at Nemours on Nov. 11, 1866 (PS 622,3). See also third instruction on the sacrifice of personality, Aug. 11, 1867 (PR 111,1 and 2). Similarly, a month before his death, he told the Sisters at Angers on July 2, 1868 (PS 642,3): "Ah! my sisters, give your personality to the Lord, then you'll be perfect, you'll be able to say with St. Paul: *it is no longer I who live...*, then you'll be very blessed, very rich."

[172] In this Lucan verse the meaning of Jesus' departure for Jerusalem as an "exodus" is clearer in the Greek.

[173] Third instruction of a retreat preached to his religious on the sacrifice of personality, Aug. 11, 1867 (PR 111,2). Earlier, on his return journey after his long Roman retreat

when stopping off at her home in Lyons (Apr. 8-11, 1865) Eymard had confided to Madame Natalie Jordan what the vow of personality meant. Since their meeting in 1846, when she joined the Third Order of Mary, this lady staunchly supported Father Eymard in following his Eucharistic vocation, whereas she herself, his "elder daughter of our Lord in his new kingdom of the Blessed Sacrament," had been encouraged on her path to holiness by his spiritual guidance through some 80 letters from 1850 to 1868. See Guitton, op. cit., pp. 268ff.

[174] It is interesting to note that his insight is similar to that proposed in the spiritual classic by Jean Pierre de Caussade, S.J. (1675-1751), *L'Abandon à la divine Providence*, edited by P.H. Ramière (Paris: Ruffet, 1861), 5th ed. 1867. Eymard refers to this in a letter to Virginie Danion on June 26, 1867 (CO 1979).

[175] His second meditation on Feb. 1, 1865, which he considered most important (NR 44,15). Cave has shown that the real issue underlying Eymard's view of the virtue of religion had been that of the significance of Christ's reign, regarding which he had for some time shared de Cuers' royalist leanings and militarist approach about the meaning of rendering a cultic service to the Real Presence of Christ in the Eucharist, but which was also the root cause of tension between Eymard and his first companion. Cf. *The "Writings,"* op. cit., pp. 91ff. Clearly, however, Eymard didn't in any way disparage the virtue of religion, for this is the fundamental attitude of worship required of every human being, leave alone Christians; cf. St. Thomas Aquinas, *S.T.* IIa IIae, q. 81, a. 2-4. Cf. also John Saward, "The Virtue of Art and the Virtue of Religion" in *The Beauty of Holiness and the Holiness of Beauty: Art, Sanctity and the Truth of Catholicism* (San Francisco: Ignatius Press, 1997), p. 76.

[176] Second instruction on the spirit of penance, Aug. 11, 1867 (PR 110,2).

[177] Many times he had spoken of the cenacle, one of the earliest of these being in his letter on Dec. 26, 1843 to his friend the Abbé Brammerel, to whom he stated that when a person discovers this it is "paradise on earth" (CO 40,1). But he first mentioned his insight about becoming an "interior cenacle" in a letter on January 8, 1864 to Madame Jordan whom he asks to pray for him to receive this grace as the "best wishes" she could give him for the New Year (CO 1334,1).

[178] It is interesting to note, however, that although he had made the complete gift of himself in the Vow of Personality, he didn't to the end of his life relinquish his cherished longing for the Jerusalem Cenacle, as evident in his heartfelt cry in the closing words of his sermon on Pentecost Sunday, May 31, 1868: "The Cenacle today in the hands of the Turks! His Cenacle. And our Lord lets this be! Children of a family buy back their paternal house to remember their ancestors.... I would die happy if I were to see a throne in the Cenacle!" (PP 61,3) See also his words in the Paris chapel on July 5, 1867 (PP 33,5): "The day when we'll have the Cenacle, I'll go around Europe, if it must be barefoot bearing a staff, to beg everywhere for help to build a magnificent temple at the Cenacle. And on that day I'll be the happiest of men."

[179] As Pope Benedict XVI put it in CV, nn. 34, 37, 28. See Justin Chawkan, S.S.S., "Eucharistic Implications in *Caritas in Veritate*," in *Emmanuel Magazine*, Vol. 116, No. 2 (March/April 2010).

[180] Conference on the second day of the Retreat at Nemours, Nov. 6, 1866 (PS 606,1). See also his instruction to novices (PR 18,18) where he quotes St. Gregory of Nyssa: "Prayer is conversion and exchanging words with God" (*De orat. Dom.*). Citing Ph 3:20 (Vulgate tr. "conversatio"), Eymard often pointed out that thanks to the Eucharist, the beginning of heaven on earth, it becomes possible to colloquy

with the Lord. Cf. e.g., May 28, 1850, Corpus Christi (PT 77,1); Dec. 18, 1860 (PS 290,2); May 25, 1861, Feast of the Ascension (PP 13,6).

181 See the conference "being serious-minded" in his last retreat to his religious on Aug. 13, 1867 (PR 117,1).

182 See his sermon published as an article, "Le siècle de l'Eucharistie," in the first issue (July, 1864) of a monthly periodical he started, *Le Très-Saint Sacrement* (PG 241,4).

183 See the *Directoire des Agrégés,* Chapter 1 (RA 18,2).

184 He presented this to Eymard; see Guitton, op. cit., p. 190.

185 "Gwen John in Paris" in *The Poems of Rowan Williams*, op. cit., p. 25.

186 As Peter Brown says in *The World of Late Antiquity* (London: Thames and Hudson, 1971), p. 74.

187 He was perhaps influenced in this regard by what he had read during his Marist formative years in the classic by Jean-Nicolas Grou, S.J. (1731-1803), *Manual for Interior Souls*. Cf. especially chapter LVII "On the effects of Holy Communion." He recommended this work in two letters: to Stéphanie Gourd, cf. in 1855 (CO 492), and to Father Michel Chanuet, cf. on December 8, 1864 (CO 1497). The Jesuit author's work was introduced to the English-speaking world by the great connoisseur of the mystical life, Baron Friedrich von Hugel, cf. "The Spiritual Writings of Father Grou, S.J." in *The Tablet*, lxxiv (1889), pp. 990ff., 1029-31.

188 See William Johnston, S.J., who describes the importance of this in the Western and Oriental mystical tradition; cf. *The Inner Eye of Love: Mysticism and Religion* (London: Collins [Fount], 1981).

189 See the monthly retreat to the Servants at Angers on June 12, 1865, less than three months after his "conversion" in the Roman retreat (cf. PS 543,1).

190 *The Everlasting Gospel.*

191 For instance: to members of the Third Order of Mary on Jan. 25, 1848 (PT 40,3), and on Apr. 4, 1848 (PT 43,1). Cf. also conference on Sept. 20, 1849: "Simplicity is the mother of all the virtues… makes everything easy… confers great peace to the heart" (PT 69,1); or where he spoke of simplicity ensuring interior union with God, May 19, 1855 (PT 97,4); effects of simplicity on a person, Sept. 19, 1849 (PT 144,2); without simplicity prayer is without fruits (PA 87,2).

192 See the last annual retreat preached to his religious in Paris, Aug. 13, 1867 (PR 116,1); or his conference in Paris to the Sister Servants where he cites also Jesus' words to Nicodemus, Sept. 7, 1860 (PS 258,3).

193 See Pope Benedict XVI on "The Eucharistic Form of the Christian Life," SCar, Part III, nn. 70ff. On the "seeing of the form," see Hans Urs von Balthasar, *The Glory of the Lord*, Vol. I [ET] (Edinburgh: T & T Clark, 1982), especially pp. 571ff.

194 Letter on June 26, 1856 (CO 599,1). In this letter he thanks this lady for her gift to this first Eucharistic cenacle.

195 See the conference on Holy Communion, nourishment and strengthening energy of the life of perfection to the Sisters at Angers on Oct. 24, 1865 (PS 546,1).

196 See *Enarr. in Ps* 98, 9: "No one eats this Flesh (which Jesus received from the flesh of the Virgin Mary) without first adoring it… Not only do we not sin by adoring it, but we would sin if we failed to worship it…" There is no dearth of evidence that a similar reverential worship for the divine Sacrament was taught by many Fathers of the Church. Cf. e.g.: St. Cyril of Jerusalem, *Cat. Myst.*, V, 21.

[197] As repeatedly stated since the Second Vatican Council, cf. e.g., Pope Benedict XVI, SCar, nn. 3, 17, 64, etc.

[198] This couldn't be more clearly stated than in his catechesis during the retreat given at Tarare in Jan. 1862 (PD 27,10). See also a similar teaching in a retreat preparatory to inaugurating perpetual exposition at Rouen in June 1860 (PD 25,12).

[199] Pope Benedict XVI pointed out the intrinsic relationship between Eucharistic celebration and Eucharistic adoration. See SCar, n. 66.

[200] *"Cor ad cor loquitur"* – the motto on Cardinal Newman's escutcheon.

[201] "Newman and the Second Vatican Council" (1966), paper given at *Rediscovery of Newman: An Oxford Symposium*. Online: http://vatican2voice.org/writes/newman.asp.

[202] Address to participants at the Cardinal Newman Academic Symposium (April 7, 1975), citing Wilfrid Ward, *The Life of John Henry Cardinal Newman,* Vol. 2 (London, 1912), p. 202.

[203] Benedict XVI, Meditation at Prayer Vigil in Hyde Park, London, on the eve of Newman's Beatification, Sept. 18, 2010, *Heart Speaks Unto Heart: Pope Benedict XVI in the UK* (London: DLT, 2010), pp. 86, 87, 88.

[204] See J.H. Newman, "Chapter X: Conversion of Augustine," in *The Church of the Fathers* (London: Burns, Oates, and Company, 1868), p. 251.

[205] Ibid., p. 255.

[206] Ibid., pp. 256ff. The passage Newman quotes is from the *Confessions*, Bk. IV.

[207] Cf. Roderick Strange, *John Henry Newman: A Mind Alive* (London: DLT, 2008), pp. 138f.

[208] Newman's friendships are well documented in Ian Ker's splendid work, *John Henry Newman: A Biography* (Oxford/New York: OUP, 2009); first publ. 1988. In the "Afterword" Ker quashes the churlish insinuations and controversy fomented by the media regarding Newman's friendship with his fellow Oratorian, Ambrose St. John. Cf. ibid., p. 747.

[209] Cf. Ian Ker (Ed.), *Apologia Pro Vita Sua: Being a History of his Religious Opinions* (Penguin, 2004), p. 23. See also Sermon 12 on "Mission of St. Philip Neri" (Pt. II) in *Sermons Preached on Various Occasions*, 1908, p. 230. Cf. also a Christmas Sermon on "Christian Sympathy" in *Parochial and Plain Sermons* [henceforth PPS] (San Francisco, CA: Ignatius Press, 1997), pp. 1039f. The Carmelite Jewish convert martyr of Auschwitz Edith Stein, a great devotee of Newman, replied with this phrase when asked about her spiritual state; in this she was following the advice of St. John of the Cross. Cf. Joanne Mosley, *Edith Stein: Woman of Prayer* (Leominster, U.K.: Gracewing, 2004), p. 72.

[210] "Moral Effects of Communion with God," in PPS, p. 884.

[211] Ibid., pp. 878, 879f. [Italics in the text.] He quotes here St. Paul's phrase: "Our conversation is in heaven" (Ph 3:20). "Conversation" in the AV is rendered "commonwealth" in the RSV.

[212] "Desire" is the key word in St. Augustine's Letter to Proba on prayer (*Epistola 130*); it occurs no less than sixty times.

[213] Sermon on "Moral Effects of Communion with God" in PPS, pp. 880f.

[214] Cf. Owen Chadwick, *Acton and History* (Cambridge: CUP, 1998), pp. 126, 138. Cf. also Hugh MacDougall, O.M.I., *The Acton-Newman Relations: The Dilemma of Christian Liberalism* (New York: Fordham University Press, 1962), pp. 140ff. Acton

referred to Newman in his *Lectures on Modern History* (London: Macmillan and Co., 1921), pp. 11, 21, 278. Acton had an influence on the writing of the *Apologia*, cf. Rocco Pezzimenti, *The Political Thought of Lord Acton. The English Catholics in the Nineteenth Century* (Leominster/Rome: Gracewing, 2001), p. 83.

215 As he says in "Knowledge viewed in relation to Religious Duty" in *The Idea of a University* (London: Longmans, Green, and Co., 1907), p. 209.

216 Cf. his poem, "The Handsome Heart."

217 PPS, pp. 259-264.

218 Sermon on "Christian Reverence" in PPS, p. 194.

219 Cf. Sermon on "Love of Relations and Friends" in PPS, p. 262. The sermon was preached on the Feast of St. John the Evangelist (the "Beloved Disciple").

220 Ibid. in PPS, p. 260.

221 Sermon on "The Thought of God, the Stay of the Soul" in PPS, p. 1160.

222 Ibid., p. 1165.

223 See his sermon at Whitsun (Pentecost), "The Communion of Saints," in PPS, pp. 839ff. Cf. also his sermon "A Home for the Lonely" in PPS, pp. 850ff.

224 Cf. *A Spiritual Aeneid* (London/New York: Longmans, Green and Co., 1918), p. 37. Browning's poem in fact concerns Wordsworth's abandonment of the Liberal Cause and his youthful democratic high idealism of radical republican sympathies with the French Revolution.

225 Cf. ibid., p. 195. Knox remarks that when it came to the time of his own turning Romeward: "I was describing the loneliness of a soul forced by conscientious motives to detach itself from loved surroundings and familiar friendships, and launch out into the deep." (Ibid., p. 226.)

226 See Sermon 26 (preached on Sept. 25, 1843) in *Sermons Bearing on Subjects of the Day* (London: Longmans, Green, and Co., 1902), pp. 395ff.

227 Barberi (1792-1849), who had received many converts into full communion with the Catholic Church, was beatified by Pope Paul VI during the Second Vatican Council on Oct. 27, 1963.

228 *Apologia*, op. cit., p. 44.

229 Sermon on "The Invisible World" in PPS, p. 860. [Italics in the text.]

230 Sermon on "Watching" in PPS, p. 946.

231 Poem CLXXV in *Prayers, Verses and Devotions* (San Francisco, CA: Ignatius Press, 2000), pp. 688f.

232 *The Christian Year, Septuagesima*, cited by John Macquarrie in his book that takes its title from a phrase in this stanza, *Two Worlds are Ours: An Introduction to Christian Mysticism* (London: SCM Press, 2004), title page and pp. 16, 221.

233 *Prayers*, op. cit., p. 689.

234 Ibid., Introduction, pp. xix, xxiv.

235 See his sermon on "Human Responsibility, as Independent of Circumstances" (November 4, 1832) in *Fifteen Sermons Preached Before the University of Oxford Between A.D. 1826 and 1843* (New York: OUP, 2006), pp. 101ff.

236 Cf. CCC nn. 2091-2092.

237 Sermon on "The Power of the Will" in PPS, p. 1184.

238 Sermon on "Promising without Doing" in PPS, p. 110.

239 Cf. Discourse 11 on "Faith and Doubt" in *Discourses to Mixed Congregations* (London: Longmans, Green, and Co., 1906), p. 226.

240 Cf. sermon on "Christ, a Quickening Spirit" (Easter Day) in PPS, p. 322.

241 Sermon 1 "The Omnipotence of God the Reason for Faith and Hope" (January 30, 1848) in *Faith and Prejudice and Other Unpublished Sermons* (New York: Sheed & Ward, 1956), pp. 27, 29.

242 Wiseman's article on the "Anglican Claim" in the *Dublin Review* (Aug. 1839). The words are from the first of Augustine's anti-Donatist writings (c. 400 A.D.), a reply to a schismatic bishop of Carthage (*Contra epistolam Parmeniani*, Lib. III, Ch. 4.24): "Quapropter securus judicat orbis terrarum, bonos non esse qui se devidunt ab orbe terrarum" [Wherefore, the entire world judges with security that they are not good who separate themselves from the entire world]. Newman alludes to having read Wiseman's article in *Certain Difficulties Felt by Anglicans in Catholic Teaching*, Vol. I (London: Longmans, Green and Co., 1909), p. 373.

243 *Apologia*, op. cit., p. 116. Cf. Augustine, *Conf.*, VIII.12 (29). Ker remarks that this passage is "one of the most dramatic and powerful in all Newman's writings and worthy of that fateful moment" (*John Henry Newman*, op. cit., pp. 182f.). Elsewhere Ker draws attention to other occasions when Newman has recourse to Augustine's phrase. Cf. Ker, "Newman, the Councils, and Vatican II," in *Communio* 28 (Winter, 2001), pp. 708ff.

244 *Apologia*, op. cit., p. 117.

245 Ibid.

246 Ibid. It is interesting that here he sees a cleavage between "reason" and "imagination" – the latter probably meaning wishful feelings, untested inclinations.

247 Cf. ibid., p. 118. Sleep, as Hopkins stated, is the easy option out of mental anguish:

> O the mind, mind has mountains; cliffs of fall
> Frightful, sheer, no-man fathomed. Hold them cheap
> May who ne'er hung there. Nor does long our small
> Durance deal with that steep or deep. Here! Creep,
> Wretch, under a comfort serves in a whirlwind: all
> Life death does end and each day dies with sleep.
> (Sonnet "No worst, there is none. Pitched past pitch of grief.")

248 *Apologia*, op. cit., p. 195.

249 The first four chapters deal with "the history of my religious opinions…," the fifth treats "the position of my mind since 1845"; cf. *Apologia*, op. cit., pp. 23ff., 51ff., 96ff., 141ff.; 214ff.

250 "Integral Evangelization" in *Josephinum*, Vol. 13, No. 1 (Winter/Spring 2006), Online: www.pcj.edu/journal/essays/nichols13-1.htm#2.

251 Cf. *Apologia*, op. cit., p. 118.

252 Ibid., p. 214.

253 Sermon (the feast of the Ascension) on "Warfare the Condition of Victory" in PPS, pp. 1330f. [Italics in the text.] May the word "Victory" in the title of this sermon be seen also as an allusion to the name of Nelson's ship at the battle of Trafalgar (Oct. 21 1805)? While he certainly deplored the insular attitudes of his fellow countrymen, which give rise to prejudice against all that is "not English," Newman was proud to be an Englishman without succumbing to narrow nationalism. Cf. Ker, *John Henry Newman*, op. cit., pp. 364ff.

254 These words are quoted by a confrere at the Birmingham Oratory; cf. Henry James Jennings, *Cardinal Newman: The Story of His Life* (London: Simpkin, Marshall and Co., 1882), p. 151.

255 Cf. *Prayers*, op. cit., p. 718.

256 Preface to his English translation of the *Catena Aurea: Commentary on the Four Gospels collected out of the works of the Fathers*, Volume I, St. Matthew (Southampton, U.K.: The Saint Austin Press, 1997), p. i.

257 Written during his European tour, off Zante, December 28, 1832, *Verses on Various Occasions* (London: Burns, Oates & Co., 1880), p. 98.

258 Sermon on "The Shepherd of Our Souls" in PPS, p. 1706.

259 *An Essay in Aid of a Grammar of Assent* (London: Longmans, Green, and Co., 1903), Ch. 9 "The Illative Sense," p. 344.

260 A special performance of Elgar's *Oratorio*, on the score of which Elgar wrote that he had given "the best of him," took place on the eve of Cardinal Newman's beatification (Sept. 18, 2010) in Birmingham Town Hall.

261 The poet T.S. Eliot's poem "Gerontion" is similar to Newman's epic only in the name. It deals with reminiscences of an old man as summed up in the last line: "Thoughts of a dry brain in a dry season."

262 At the time of writing this poem Newman was engaged in intense reflection about the meaning of his life and the eventual approach of death. This is indicated in the following words: "I write at once... because I do not know how long this perfect possession of my sensible and available health and strength may last." (Words "written in prospect of death" on Passion Sunday, Mar. 13, 1864 "at 7 o'clock a.m."), "Meditations and Devotions" in *Prayers*, op. cit., p. 445. See also other subsequent notes he wrote giving instructions about his burial and the inscription on his tombstone (July 23, 1876 and Feb. 13, 1881); cf. ibid., p. 447.

263 As cited by Arthur L. Clements, *Poetry of Contemplation: John Donne, George Herbert, Henry Vaughan, and the Modern Period* (Albany, NY: State University of New York Press, 1990), p. 165. [Italics in the text.]

264 Discourse 4 "Purity and Love" in *Discourses*, op. cit., p. 67.

265 *Letters to Malcolm Chiefly on Prayer* (Collins Fontana Books, 1966), p. 110.

266 As suggested by Maurice F. Egan; cf. Introduction to *The Dream of Gerontius* (New York: Cosimo Inc., 2007), p. 9.

267 Cf. *Macbeth*, Act II, Sc. II.

268 "The Rime of the Ancient Mariner," Pt V.

269 *The Portal of the Mystery of Hope*, op. cit., p. 126.

270 *The Dream of Gerontius*, in *Prayers*, op. cit., p. 717.

271 Ibid., p. 691.

272 *Holy Sonnets*, No. 10.

273 *The Dream of Gerontius*, in *Prayers*, op. cit., p. 691.

274 Ibid., p. 722.

275 "Gerontius' Dream" in *Emmanuel*, Vol. 116, No. 6 (Nov.-Dec. 2010), p. 503, citing the words of Noel D. O'Donoghue, O.D.C.

276 *The Dream of Gerontius*, in *Prayers*, op. cit., p. 718.

277 Newman may have known Samuel Crossman's hymn "My Song is Love Unknown," which was published in *The Young Man's Meditation*, or *Some Few Sacred Poems*

upon Select Subjects and Scriptures (originally printed by J.H. for S. Thompson, 1664) in 1863 by Daniel Sedgwich.

278 *The Dream of Gerontius*, in *Prayers*, op. cit., p. 694. This prayer of Gerontius has become the hymn "Firmly I believe and truly" in *The Westminster Hymnal* (London: Burns & Oates, 1965), no. 185 p. 199.

279 Ibid.

280 Discourse 13: "Mysteries of Nature and of Grace" in *Discourses*, op. cit., p. 269.

281 Discourse 4: "Purity and Love" in ibid., p. 70.

282 *Certain Difficulties Felt by Anglicans in Catholic Teaching*, Vol. II, op. cit., pp. 31ff.

283 *An Essay on the Development of Christian Doctrine* (Notre Dame, IN: University of Notre Dame Press), Introduction, p. 6. Similar statements are found throughout the argument of this work; cf. ibid., Ch. II, Sect. II, 8, p. 82.

284 *Apologia*, op. cit., Chapter V, p. 214.

285 Ibid., p. 215.

286 See his sermon "Illuminating Grace" (Discourse 9 in *Discourses to Mixed Congregations* (Longmans, Green, and Co., 1906), p. 191; also his sermon on "Faith and Doubt" (Discourse 11 in ibid., p. 226).

287 *Apologia*, op. cit., p. 38. [Italics in the text.]

288 Ibid. [Italics in the text.]

289 *An Essay on the Grammar of Assent*, op. cit., p. 352.

290 Cf. ibid., Ch. 9, pp. 343ff.

291 Cf. Ian Ker, *The Achievement of John Henry Newman* (Notre Dame, IN: University of Notre Dame Press, 1990), pp. 50ff.

292 *Development of Christian Doctrine*, op. cit., p. 5.

293 Cf. Ker, *John Henry Newman*, op. cit., p. 287. Aidan Nichols gives a detailed account of the background development of Newman's treatment of the issue through his Anglican days to his Catholic period. Cf. *From Newman to Congar: The Idea of Doctrinal Development from the Victorians to the Second Vatican Council* (Edinburgh: T & T Clark, 1990), pp. 17ff.

294 *Certain Difficulties Felt by Anglicans in Catholic Teaching*, Vol. I (London: Longmans, Green and Co., 1909), Lecture 12: "Ecclesial History: No Prejudice to the Apostolicity of the Church," p. 368.

295 Ibid., pp. 394f.

296 *Development of Christian Doctrine*, op. cit., Ch. 1, Section 1 (end), p. 40.

297 Nichols, *From Newman to Congar*, op. cit., p. 49 (citing Paul Misner).

298 *The Emergence of the Catholic Tradition (100-600)* (Chicago and London: University of Chicago Press, 1975), p. 9.

299 "Fides quaerens intellectum," cf. *Proslogion*.

300 Cf. Sermon 15 on "The theory of developments in religious doctrine" in Newman's University Sermons. *Fifteen Sermons*, op. cit., pp. 211ff.

301 Ker chastises the post-Christian biographer Robert Bernard Martin for giving "a purely psychological interpretation" of Hopkins' disappointment, not taking "religion seriously as a powerful motivating force in a person's life." See Ker, "John Henry Newman and Gerard Manley Hopkins," Online: www.gerardmanleyhopkins. org/ Lectures_2007/hopkins _and_newman.html.

302 These contrasting emotions are well evidenced in his "nature" poetry (such as "God's grandeur" or "That Nature is a Heraclitean Fire") and in his "Terrible Sonnets."

303 As he explained to Robert Bridges, cf. *The Letters of Gerard Manley Hopkins to Robert Bridges* (London: OUP, 1955), 2nd ed., p. 188.

304 Cited by Ker in "John Henry Newman and Gerard Manley Hopkins," *The Letters*, 1973, viii. 166,

305 "Hymne to God, my God, in my sicknesse," *The 'Divine' Poems*, OUP (Ed. Helen Gardner), 1982, p. 50.

306 John Henry Newman, *Lectures on the Prophetical Office of the Church, Via Media*, Vol. I (London: Longmans, Green, and Co., 1901), p. 13.

307 Cited by Ker, *John Henry Newman*, op. cit., p. 522.

308 Cited in ibid., p. 520.

309 Cf. Strange, op. cit., Chapter: "Strange Providence," pp. 109f.

310 "Meditations and Devotions" in *Prayers*, op. cit., pp. 338f.

311 Words to Father Ambrose St. John in 1862, cited in Meriol Trevor's Introduction to *Meditations and Devotions* (London: Burns & Oates, 1964), p. vii.

312 Chapter thus entitled in Ker, *John Henry Newman*, op. cit., pp. 490ff.

313 *Sermons* 1824-1843, vol. I, 1991, Sermons on the Liturgy and the Sacraments and on Christ the Mediator, p. 91. [Italics in the text.]

314 *Grammar of Assent*, op. cit., Ch. 10, p. 464.

315 Nicholai Vassilyevich Gogol (1809-1852) Introduction to *The Divine Liturgy of the Russian Orthodox Church* [ET by Rosemary Edmonds] (London: Darton, Longman & Todd, 1960), p. xvi.

316 Cf. Post-synodal Apostolic Exhortation *Evangelii nuntiandi* (Dec. 8. 1975), 42.

317 "Little Gidding" IV. This, the fourth and last of *Four Quartets*, was written and appeared first in *The New English Weekly* on Oct. 15, 1942, during the horrendous bombing of London.

318 *The Dream of Gerontius*, in *Prayers*, op. cit., p. 721. Nichols draws attention to the phrase "higher gift than grace" as reflecting the leitmotif of Matthias Scheeben's teaching on the supernatural; cf. Nichols, *Scribe of the Kingdom: Essays on Theology and Culture*, Vol. 1 (London: Sheed & Ward, 1994), p. 210. This great Rhineland theologian's kernel insight, which is becoming appreciated today, is in many respects similar to Newman's repeated emphasis, namely, that the mysteries of God in Revelation should be the main focus in guiding the use of philosophy in theological endeavor. In this way "faith seeking understanding" will once again come into its own as in the days of the Fathers.

319 See, for instance, his sermon on "Mysteries of Nature and Grace" in *Discourses*, op. cit., pp. 260ff.

320 Cf. Ker, *John Henry Newman*, op. cit., p. 49. Ker suggests that Newman's assimilation of the Fathers' notion of "economy" or "dispensation" is the most interesting feature of his first book, *The Arians of the Fourth Century*.

321 *Apologia*, op. cit., p. 479, Appendix 7.

322 Cf. ibid., pp. 240, 306f., 316, 480f., 495. The theory that the early Christian discipline derived from the mystery religions has been largely discredited. The liturgical theologian Josef Jungmann says that the "disciplina arcani" cannot be proved to

have existed prior to the 3rd century. Cf. *The Early Liturgy* [ET] (London: DLT, 1963), p. 159. Edward Yarnold, S.J. says there is only little evidence of it before the middle of the 4th century and after the middle of the 5th it fell out of use; cf. *The Study of the Liturgy* (London: SPCK, 1979), pp. 109f.

323 *Apologia*, op. cit., p. 479.

324 Cf. e.g., *LG*, Ch. II, 16 and n. 20 referring to Eusebius of Caesarea, *Praeparatio Evangelica*, I.1; Decree on the Church's Missionary Activity, *Ad Gentes* (Dec. 7, 1965), Ch. I, 3 and n. 2 with references to many Church Fathers.

325 St. Irenaeus of Lyons developed this theme in *Adv. Haer.*, III.16.6. Ker quotes Newman's words about longing for the summer vacation to get back to his patristic studies: "I am so hungry for Irenaeus and Cyprian," Ker, *John Henry Newman*, op. cit., p. 35.

326 Cf. sermon on "Purity and Love," in *Discourses*, op. cit., p. 78. While using the phrase "wound in the soul" in describing Mary Magdalene, Newman applies it also to St. Augustine and St. Ignatius Loyola.

327 *The Dream of Gerontius*, in *Prayers*, op. cit., p. 717.

328 Cf. St. John of the Cross, *The Living Flame of Love*; St. Teresa of Avila, *The Interior Castle*, Ch. II. See also the 14th century English mystic Julian of Norwich, *Revelations of Divine Love*, Ch. 2.

329 Cf. *Grammar of Assent*, op. cit., Ch. 10, p. 425. On the title page of this work he quotes St. Ambrose's words about God not employing a method of dialectic in offering salvation.

330 Ibid., Ch. 4, pp. 94f. [Italics in text.] Newman quotes his own words written earlier (February 1841) as a protest against what had been proposed by Lord Brougham and Sir Robert Peel. Cf. *Discussions and Arguments on Various Subjects* (London: Longmans, Green, and Co., 1907), IV, pp. 254ff.

331 Johnston, *The Wounded Stag* (Collins Fount Paperbacks, 1985), p. 17; cf. St. John of the Cross, *The Spiritual Canticle*, Stanza 13. Applying the imagery of the wounded stag to the Eucharist, Johnston states that this is "the principal source of Christian religious experience and Christian mystical experience" (p. 78).

332 Cf. PPS, pp. 1230ff. and Sermon 16 in *Discourses*, op. cit., pp. 323ff. Cf. Ker, 1993 pp. 28ff.

333 Sermon on "The Visible Church for the Sake of the Elect" in PPS, pp. 828f.

334 Sermon on "The Visible Church for the Sake of the Elect" in PPS, pp. 834f.

335 See "University Preaching" in *The Idea of a University*, 1907, pp. 406, 408ff.

336 Discourse 1 on "The Salvation of the Hearer the Motive of the Preacher" in *Discourses*, op. cit., p. 18. This collection was Newman's first published work as a Roman Catholic priest.

337 Discourse 12: "Prospects of the Catholic Missioner" in ibid., p. 246. He gave this sermon at the opening of the London Oratory on May 31, 1849.

338 Ibid., p. 258. When criticized for over-severity he retorted that his model was the great giver of missions in Italy and exemplary teacher of a moderate approach in moral theology, St. Alphonsus de Liguori, the Founder of the Redemptorists, whose motto was *Copiosa apud eum est redemptio* ("With him there is plentiful redemption" Ps 129[130]:7), cf. Ker, 2009, p. 342.

339 "University Preaching" in *The Idea of a University*, 1907, pp. 407f.

340 Cf. e.g., his Sermon on "Self-Contemplation" in PPS, pp. 331ff.

341 Sermon on "Promising without Doing" in PPS, pp. 170f. This sermon is on the parable about the difference between two sons, the one who did and the other failed to carry out their father's will (cf. Mt 21:28-30). [Italics in the text.]

342 Cf. Sermon on "The Christian Ministry" in PPS, pp. 418ff. The characteristics of witness, dispenser, overseer and intercessor were brought out by Michael Ramsey, cf. Rowan Williams, "The Christian Priest Today" (lecture given at Cuddesdon to mark the centenary of Ramsey's birth, Nov. 14, 1904), in *Glory Descending: Michael Ramsey and His Writings* (Grand Rapids, MI/Cambridge, UK: William B. Eerdmans Publishing Co., 2005), pp. 163ff.

343 See Sermon on "Self-Denial the Test of Religious Earnestness" in PPS, p. 71: "There are such imperfections, such inconsistencies in the heart and life of even the better sort of men, that continual repentance must ever go hand in hand with our endeavors to obey. Much we need the grace of Christ's blood to wash us from the guilt we daily incur; much need we the aid of His promised Spirit!"

344 Quoted from one of his letters by Ker in a chapter on preaching; cf. Ker, 1990, p. 77.

345 Sermon 7 on "Sins of Ignorance and Weakness" in PPS, p. 62.

346 As Ker observes, referring to Newman's sermon on "The Spiritual Mind" (cf. PPS, p. 50), cf. Ker, 1990, p. 91.

347 Sermon on "Watching" in PPS, pp. 938ff.

348 Sermon on "Waiting for Christ" (27th Sunday after Pentecost, 1856) in *Sermons Preached on Various Occasions*, 1908, p. 33.

349 Cf. Ker, 1990, pp. 90f. Ker also suggests here an interesting comparison between this point and what Newman also learned from his Evangelical background, namely, that while he was opposed to a judgmental attitude dichotomizing "nominal" and "real" Christians, Newman derived from it his famous distinction of "notional" and "real" assent, so crucial in his approach to spirituality.

350 Cf. *Hamlet*, Act I, Sc. iii: "This above all: to thine own self be true." This echoes the Greek aphorism of Delphi: "Know thyself"; see e.g. Plato, *Protagoras*, 343b; Diogenes Laertius, I.xl.

351 Augustine's aim was to know God inscribed in the truth of himself, as he expressed it in his prayer: "Noverim me, noverim te," *Soliloquies*, II, 1,1; cf. also *Conf.*, VII, 10, 16.

352 Sermon on "Sins of Infirmity" in PPS, p. 1093.

353 Cf. his sermon on "Holiness Necessary for Future Blessedness" in PPS, pp. 5ff.

354 Cf. Caldecott, *Beauty for Truth's Sake*, op. cit., pp. 28f.

355 *Newman* (New York: Meridian Books, 1960), p. 83.

356 The relationship of these recurring themes is set out by Roderick Strange, who notes rightly, nevertheless, that this ought not to constrict our understanding of Newman's thought into the straitjacket of a theory. For, as Strange puts it well: "While mapping the mind, we must never forget the man. The man was always more interested in reality than theory." (Strange, op. cit., p. 32.)

357 Sermon 6 "The Mind of Children" in PPS, p. 64.

358 This hardly merits Lytton Strachey's comment apropos his belief in the miraculous transfer of the house of Loreto: "When Newman was a child he 'wished that he could believe the Arabian Nights were true.' When he came to be a man, his wish seems to have been granted." Strachey, *Eminent Victorians: Cardinal Manning,*

Florence Nightingale, Dr. Arnold, General Gordon (London: Chatto and Windus, 1918), p. 29.

[359] Cf. Post-synodal Apostolic Exhortation *Verbum Domini* (Sept. 30, 2010), n. 51. "Contemporaneity" is a better translation of "Identitas temporis" of the Latin text of this document than "relevance," which mistranslates the sense of the Latin.

[360] *Change in Focus: A Study of Doctrinal Change and Continuity* (London: Sheed & Ward, 1973), p. 162.

[361] In the seven rules he gives for writing sermons the salient point is his emphasis of simplicity and humility to ensure communication between preacher and listeners. Cf. Newman, *Favorite Newman Sermons* (1932), p. 414.

[362] Such was Matthew Arnold's recollection in the third lecture he delivered in America. Cf. *Discourses in America* (London: Macmillan, 1885), cited by Joseph A. Munitiz and Oonagh Walker, "Glimpses of Newman 1801-1890" in *The Way*, No. 40 (Oct. 2010), p. 9.

[363] Apart from some longer discourses he gave on various occasions, such as the famous "Second Spring" given at the First Provincial Synod of Westminster at Oscott in 1852.

[364] *Cor ad cor loquitur* and *Ex umbris et imaginibus in veritatem*.

[365] In 1855 he had quoted a similar phrase from St. Francis de Sales ("sanè cor cordi loquitur") in a public letter on university preaching, revised and published in *The Idea of a University*; cf. Ker, 2009, p. 719.

[366] *Prayers*, op. cit., p. 428.

[367] Cf. ibid., p. 447. In many a sermon he waxed eloquent on the contrast between the shadowy aspect of this life and the reality revealed by God; cf., e.g., Sermon on "Faith without sight" in PPS, p. 239: "shadows and deceits of this shifting scene of time and sense."

[368] One may be Origen's teaching about the transition from this world's shadows and images to Christ's revelation of the truth and reality of eternal life; cf. *Com. Rom.* 1,4; *Frag. Io.*, 9.12; *De Prin.* IV, 1, 6. More probably, however, it may well be a sentence in St. Ambrose, whom Newman greatly revered: "There is a shadow in the Law, an image in the Gospel, in the last judgment truth" (*umbram in lege, imaginem in evangelio, in iudicio veritatem*); cf. Ambrose, *Funeral oration for his brother Satirus*, II.109. Newman quotes St. Ambrose on the title page of *A Grammar of Assent* (see above note 329), and mentions this Father among the saints through whose intercession he commits his soul and body to the Holy Trinity. Cf. "Conclusion written in prospect of death, March 13th 1864" in *Prayers*, op. cit., p. 445.

[369] This point is made in various sermons; cf. e.g., on "The Gospel Witnesses" (Feast of St. Philip and James) in PPS, p. 350; on "The Mystery of Godliness" (Christmas) in PPS, p. 1015; on "The New Works of the Gospel" (Epiphany) in PPS, p. 1063; on "The Mystery of the Holy Trinity" (Trinity Sunday) in PPS, p. 1409.

[370] See chapters 2, 3, 4 on the value of theology and its relation to all other disciplines in Part I of *The Idea of a University*, 1907, pp. 19-98.

[371] *The Dream of Gerontius*, in *Prayers*, op. cit., p. 710.

[372] Cf. "Real Bread" in Knox, *The Pastoral Sermons of Ronald Knox* (London: Burns & Oates, 1961), p. 258. The same thought appears in other sermons, cf. e.g., ibid. pp. 203ff., 335ff. The collection of these sermons was also published in *The Window in the Wall: And Other Sermons on the Holy Eucharist* (London: Burns & Oates, 1956).

373 Cf. e.g., *Grammar of Assent*, op. cit., Ch. 5, pp. 101ff. His view may be compared with that of Pascal, cf. *Pensées*, op. cit., p. 169 [Brunschvicg 556] and p. 309, "The Memorial."

374 Coulson relays Newman's reply about the Church looking rather foolish without the laity, when Bishop Ullathorne challenged him, "Who are the laity?" Cf. John Coulson, Introduction to *On Consulting the Faithful in Matters of Doctrine* (New York: Sheed & Ward, 1961), pp. 18f. In this essay, Newman mused on Ullathorne's remark that the laity's faith is a "reflection" of the Church's teaching: "that is, the people are a *mirror*, in which the Bishops see themselves. Well, I suppose a person may *consult* his glass, and in that way may know things about himself which he can learn in no other way." Coulson, op. cit., p. 72. [Italics in the text.]

375 Cf. Cardinal Avery Dulles, S.J., "Newman in retrospect" in Dulles, *John Henry Newman* (London/New York: Continuum, 2009), pp. 150ff.

376 In Newman there is nothing of Evelyn Waugh's sarcasm, such as in the following words: "A national church, however wide the empire... could never speak with universal authority and, because it was provincial, it was necessarily narrow, finding room for scandalous doctrinal aberrations but forever incapable of enclosing the vast variety of humanity. Transplanted the Church of England became merely the church of the golf club and the garrison...," Waugh's introduction to Robert Hugh Benson's novel *Richard Raynal: Solitary* (Chicago: 1956), quoted by Pearce, *Literary Converts: Spiritual Inspiration in an Age of Unbelief* (San Francisco: Ignatius Press, 2000), p. 163.

377 See Chadwick, "Road to Rome" in *The Tablet*, Saturday Mar. 10, 2001.

378 Address on Sept. 17, 2010, at Lambeth Palace in London, the residence of the Archbishop of Canterbury – Benedict XVI, *Heart Speaks Unto Heart*, op. cit., pp. 45f.

379 A very significant phrase in the embolism after the Lord's Prayer in the Eucharistic celebration.

380 Sermon in the University Church of St. Mary the Virgin, Oxford, Thursday, Feast of the Purification, Feb.2, 1843, on "The Theory of Developments in Religious Doctrine," cf. *Fifteen Sermons*, op. cit., p. 212. In note 212 on p. 401 (ibid.) Newman's words about Mary in *Meditations and Devotions of the Late Cardinal Newman* (London, 1893, p. 48), are cited: "Must not also the knowledge which she gained during those many years from His conversation of present, past, and future, have been so large... that, though she was a poor woman without human advantages, she must in her knowledge... have excelled the greatest of philosophers, and in her theological knowledge the greatest of theologians...?"

381 See Pope John Paul II, Encyclical Letter *Ut Unum Sint*, May 25, 1995, 41.

382 See Sermon 10 on "Faith and Reason, Contrasted as Habits of Mind" (preached on the feast of the Epiphany 1839 at Oxford) in *Fifteen Sermons*, op. cit., p. 142, where he says that many controversies arise out of being at cross-purpose, "verbal ones; and could they be brought to a plain issue, they would be brought to a prompt termination... When men understand each other's meaning, they see, for the most part, that controversy is either superfluous or hopeless." This sermon caused no little difficulty and disturbed some to question their simplistic faith. See the Editors' Introduction to *Fifteen Sermons*, op. cit., pp. lxxxf.

383 Sermon 1 on "Intellect the Instrument of Religion" in *Sermons Preached on Various Occasions* (London: Longmans, Green, and Co., 1908), p. 5.

384 See Ch. 3: "Bearing of Theology on other Branches of Knowledge" in *The Idea of a University*, op. cit., p. 51.

385 See Ker's chapter "Newman, Councils, and Vatican II" in Ian Ker & Terrence Merrigan (Eds.), *Newman and Faith* (Leuven, Belgium: Peeters, 2004), p. 142. See also his remarks in an article "The Significance of Newman's Conversion" in *Communio*, 22 (1995), p. 445. Cf. also Jean-Marie Tillard, O.P., "Ex Tenebris Lux: Ecumenism Enters a New Phase" in *The Unity We Have and the Unity We Seek* (London/New York: T & T Clark [Continuum], 2003), p. 197.

386 See Ker, "Newman, Councils, and Vatican II," loc. cit., pp. 140f.

387 Cf. *Development of Christian Doctrine*, op. cit., pp. 35-36, 324.

388 Since the Second Vatican Council the literature on the ecclesial experience of communion has been vastly growing. See for example: J-M. Tillard, O.P., *Church of Churches: The Ecclesiology of Communion* (Collegeville, MN: The Liturgical Press, 1992); Joseph Ratzinger, *Called to Communion: Understanding the Church Today* [ET] (San Francisco, CA: Ignatius Press, 1996); David L. Schindler, *Heart of the World, Center of the Church: Communio Ecclesiology, Liberalism and Liberation* (Grand Rapids, MI/Edinburgh: Wm. B. Eerdmans Publ. Co., T & T Clark 1996); Dennis M. Doyle, *Communion Ecclesiology: Vision and Versions* (Maryknoll, NY: Orbis Books, 2000).

389 Address to the United Nations 50th General Assembly, New York, Oct. 5, 1995.

390 Interview reported Online: www.acton.org/publications/randl/rl_interview_319. php

391 *No Greater Love* (Novato, CA: New World Library, 2002), p. 103.

392 SpS, 39.

393 Title of the book by Mary Craig, *Man from a Far Country. A Portrait of Pope John Paul II* (London: Hodder and Stoughton, 1979).

394 Cf. Encyclical Letter *Ecclesia de Eucharistia* (Apr. 17, 2003), Ch. 6: "At the School of Mary, 'Woman of the Eucharist,'" nn. 53-58.

395 *Crossing the Threshold of Hope* [ET] (New York: Alfred A. Knopf, 1994), pp. 212f. [Italics in the text.]

396 See Avery Dulles, S.J., *The Splendor of Faith: The Theological Vision of Pope John Paul II* (New York: Crossroad, 1999), p. 6.

397 *Thirsting for God: A Yearbook of Prayers, Meditations, and Anecdotes,* Mother Teresa (Servant Publications: 2000), p. 134.

398 Cited in Mother Teresa, *Come be my Light: The Private Writings of the "Saint of Calcutta,"* ed. Brian Kolodiejchuk, M.C. (Doubleday, 2007), p. 42.

399 Lenten Message 1993, nn. 1 and 2 (Libreria Editrice Vaticana).

400 Encyclical Letter *Redemptor Hominis* (Mar. 4, 1979), n. 9. He devoted his entire second Encyclical Letter to the theme of the inexhaustible richness of God's merciful love, cf. *Dives in misericordia* (Nov. 30, 1980).

401 Roman Parish of St. Gelasius I on the 3rd Sunday of Lent, Mar. 3, 2002, n. 5 (Libreria Editrice Vaticana). This homily prepared by the pope was read by the Vicar General of the diocese of Rome, Cardinal Camillo Ruini.

402 This feast, which had already been celebrated in Poland and in the Vatican, was extended to the Universal Church on Apr. 30, 2000, when Pope John Paul II canonized Faustina Kowalska, a Polish nun who in a private revelation had received the mission to promote grateful recognition of the divine mercy.

Notes

403 Online: http://www.vatican.va/holy_father/john_paul_ii/homilies/2003/documents/hf_jp-ii_hom_20031019_mother-teresa_en.html

404 See the Encyclical Letter *Sollicitudo Rei Socialis* (Dec. 30, 1987).

405 DCE, n. 14.

406 EE, n. 20.

407 Ibid. [Italics in the text.]

408 Cf. *LG*, n. 1; *GS*, n. 42.

409 *Nostra Aetate* (Oct. 28, 1965), n. 2.

410 Ibid., n. 5.

411 Cf. Online: http://www.state.gov/secretary/rm/2010/02/136501.htm

412 He quotes from *GS*, n. 27.

413 EV, n. 4.

414 Ibid., n. 25. [Italics in the text.]

415 Ibid., n. 67. [Italics in the text.]

416 Ibid., n. 81.

417 Address at a General Audience on Feb. 14, 2001, nn. 1 and 4. See also his discourse on Irenaeus' rich Christological and Trinitarian theology to the Academic Body of the Catholic University in Lyons on Oct. 7, 1986.

418 "Invocation to Man Who Became the Body of History" in *The Place Within: The Poetry of Pope John Paul II* [ET] (London: Hutchinson, 1995), p. 125.

419 Ibid., p. 118.

420 "Proper Weight" in *The Place Within*, op. cit., p. 59. The imagery of "weight" may allude to St. Augustine's famous phrase: "My weight is my love," cf. above, p. 24.

421 Cf. e.g., General Audience on May 3, 2000; *L'Osservatore Romano*, 10 May 2000.

422 See his Apostolic Letter to the Superior General of the Discalced Carmelite Order on the centenary of the death of St. John of the Cross (Dec. 14, 1990), 3 and 4.

423 Cf. Muggeridge, *Something Beautiful for God* (London: Collins, 1971), pp. 17f.

424 *Mother Teresa: Come Be My Light*, op. cit., p. 1. Letter on Mar. 6, 1962, to Father Joseph Neuner, an Austrian Jesuit theologian, who taught in Indian theological colleges.

425 Cf. ibid., p. 44.

426 Ibid., p. 40.

427 See ibid., p. 20. This letter of Feb. 8, 1937, is to her former Jesuit confessor in Albania, Fr. Jambreković.

428 Ibid., pp. 2f. This undated letter (though thought to be written during her retreat of April 1961) was to Father Neuner, S.J.

429 Ibid., p. 293, Instruction to the Missionaries of Charity, Oct. 17, 1977.

430 Ibid., p. 295, Letter to Father Michael van der Peet, Oct. 18, 1980.

431 The parable is related in Fyodor Dostoevsky's *The Brothers Karamazov*, Part III, Book VII, Chapter 3.

432 As he put it in a poem, "Song of the Inexhaustible Sun," in *The Place Within*, op. cit., p. 22.

[433] *Witness to Hope* is the appropriate title of George Weigel's authoritative biography of Pope John Paul II (New York: Harper-Collins Publishers, Inc. [First Cliff Street Books] 1999), 2001.

[434] As Anthony Kelly, C.Ss.R. put it. Cf. *Eschatology and Hope* (Maryknoll, NY: Orbis Books, 2006), p. 28.

[435] As the poet G.M. Hopkins has it in a lovely phrase in "The Starlight Night."

[436] http://www.vatican.va/holy_father/benedict_xvi/homilies/2011/documents/hf_ben-xvi_hom_20110501_beatificazione-gpii_en.html

[437] *The Portal of the Mystery of Hope*, op. cit., pp. 17f.

[438] http://www.iec2012.ie/index.jsp?p=159&n=168&a=0